The Ultimate
Trans Pennine Trail Guide

Coast to Coast Across Northern England by Bike or On Foot
Southport to Hornsea

The Official Trans Pennine Trail **Guide**

EXCELLENT BOOKS

richardpeacecycling.com
richardpeace6@gmail.com
4th edition, 4th print 2024
Text & Images © Richard Peace 2024

ISBN 978 1901464 36 8

Whilst the author has researched the route for the purposes of this guide, no responsibility can be accepted for any unforeseen circumstances encountered whilst following it. The publisher would, however, welcome any information regarding any material changes and any problems encountered.

Front cover photos, clockwise from top left:
Riding the Hornsea Rail Trail
Rother Valley Country Park
Walton Colliery Country Park
Rear cover photo:
Looking back down Longdendale from the TPT as it crosses the Pennines
Frontispiece: Fish sculpture marking the start of the the TPT, Southport

CONTENTS

INTRODUCTION..4
SOUTHPORT - WIDNES 51 km / 32 miles.....................................10
WIDNES - STOCKPORT 51 km / 32 miles......................................28
STOCKPORT - PENISTONE 51 km / 32 miles................................40
PENISTONE - DONCASTER 45 km / 28 miles................................56
BARNSLEY - CHESTERFIELD 59.5 km / 37 miles..........................72
BARNSLEY - LEEDS 45 km / 28 miles..92
DONCASTER - SELBY 45 km / 28 miles.......................................106
SELBY - YORK 24 km / 15 miles..116
SELBY - ELLOUGHTON & BROUGH 45 km / 28 miles.................124
ELLOUGHTON & BROUGH - HORNSEA 42 km / 26 miles..........132
EQUESTRIAN INFORMATION..148

Introduction

What is the Trans Pennine Trail?
- The first multi-user long distance route in the country.
- A recreation and transport route, currently for walkers and cyclists, with over two-thirds available for horse riders and sections suitable for people using wheelchairs and pushchairs. The TPT website has an interactive map with descriptions of access points with measurements plus a list of accessible venues.
- A coast to coast route, linking the ports of Liverpool and Hull with connections to the seaside resorts of Southport on the Irish Sea and Hornsea on the North Sea.
- It links other major towns and cities across the North including Leeds, Wakefield, Barnsley, York, Selby, Manchester, Doncaster, Rotherham, Sheffield and Chesterfield.
- 215 miles (346km) coast to coast, with a total trail length of more than 350 miles (560km).
- Around 70% of the route avoids roads, using disused railway lines, riversides, canal towpaths and cross-country paths.
- Part of the National Cycle Network, which totals nearly 13,000 miles. The TPT links with many other cycle routes; local links include the Leeds-Liverpool canal and long distance ones the Way of the Roses Route.
- Developed by a unique partnership of 27 local authorities across the North, the trail officially opened in September 2001 following expenditure of £30m to ensure provision of a high quality route and regeneration of some previously derelict areas.
- It was the first designated European Long Distance Route for walkers in the country, linking the west of Ireland with Europe. Currently it goes as far as the Poland / Ukraine border and there is a section in Bulgaria, but it is hoped that ultimately it will end in Istanbul. (Long distance route E8).

Friends of the Trans Pennine Trail
The Friends of the Trans Pennine Trail is a voluntary body of people who pay a membership fee and want to get the most out of the trail and see it succeed. They can also help by lobbying and campaigning, practically supporting the trail project team, promoting the TPT and sometimes also being volunteer rangers (there is no financial obligation for rangers).

Maps & Transport
Three official map guides show all route options for walkers, cyclists and horseriders. Together with this guide they provide all the information trail users need, along the whole length of the trail. The maps are available separately or as a set from the Trans Pennine Trail Office (see opposite) or from all good bookshops;
Trans Pennine Trail West   Irish Sea to Yorkshire £5.95 ISBN 978-095-3227778
Trans Pennine Trail Central Derbyshire & Yorkshire £5.95 ISBN 978-095-3227785
Trans Pennine Trail East Yorkshire to North Sea £5.95 ISBN 978-095-3227792
Much of the TPT is well served by rail. The official maps show railway stations near to the trail. The two main exceptions where train transport becomes more distant are the Longdendale Trail area and the Hull-Hornsea section. The best general advice for cyclists is to book a bike space if possible (this depends on the service - note there are some peak time bans). See operators' websites for specific detail. Where bikes are carried there is no charge. Buses are handy for walkers but will normally only take folding bikes.
Please reduce environmental impact by using public transport to get to the TPT when you can. Covering a linear stretch of the route is often easier this way, and you'll be supporting local services. See the Trail & Rail Planner on pages 8-9 for an easy way to

INTRODUCTION

plan trips on the TPT using the train. Car parks are sparse on many parts of the TPT so please don't obstruct farm gates or residential access if you do come by car.

For public transport, travel information and journey planning:
National Train Information 03457 48 49 50 nationalrail.co.uk
Traveline 0871 200 2233 traveline.info
Merseyside also has merseytravel.gov.uk and Manchester has tfgm.com

Useful Contact Addresses
Trans Pennine Trail National Office c/o Barnsley Council PO Box 597 Barnsley S70 9EW
Tel: (01226) 772574 e-mail: info@transpenninetrail.org.uk   transpenninetrail.org.uk
The Ramblers 13 Dirty Lane, London SE1 9PA (020) 3961 3300 ramblers.org.uk
Sustrans 2 Cathedral Square, College Green, Bristol BS1 5DD Information Line: 0300 303 2604 or 0117 926 8893 info@sustrans.org.uk sustrans.org.uk
Cycling UK Parklands. Railton Road, Guildford. Surrey. GU2 9JX 01483 238300 cyclinguk.org
British Horse Society Abbey Park, Stareton. Kenilworth, Warwickshire CV8 2XZ
Tel: 02476 840500 bhs.org.uk
Camping & Caravanning Club Greenfields House, Westwood Way, Coventry CV4 8JH 024 7647 5448 campingandcaravanningclub.co.uk
YHA Trevelyan House Dimple Road, Matlock. Derbyshire DE4 3YH 01629 592700 yha.org.uk

TPT GUIDE

Access, Signing & User Groups

The whole of the TPT is signed both ways. The full route is for walkers and cyclists with long stretches also for horse riders. Many miles have relatively easy access suitable for some trail users with physical disabilities or families with young children.

TPT signs usually bear the two wavy lines that make up the official trail logo and much of the trail signing is in blue and white. Being part of Sustrans National Cycle Network there are often route numbers in white and red too, as the trail uses variously numbered sections of the Network.

Remember the trail is also 'braided' so that certain sections are only available (or in some cases just recommended) for walkers or cyclists or horseriders, or a combination of the three. The photo on the left illustrates how this particular section is available to all three types of trail user. Sections available to specific types of trail user are usually indicated on the signage accordingly, as with this example on the right. There are also plenty of more discreet signs; for example keep an eye on signposts, lamposts and gates that may bear TPT stickers or plaques to confirm you are on the right track (see below left and below centre).

Where temporary diversions are in place there may also be temporary route stickers in yellow and black (see below right).

INTRODUCTION

Enjoy the Trail - User Code

The Trans Pennine Trail is a route for walkers, cyclists and in parts, horseriders who often share the same route. To keep everybody safe and happy every effort has been made to create a route suitable for all permitted users. But enjoyment of the Trans Pennine Trail relies on everybody showing consideration to each other.
Please follow the sensible guidelines in our User Code when you are on the Trail.

All users
If paths or sides of the path are signed for different user groups please keep to your side.
If you are in a group, please do not walk or ride across the whole width of the path, leave space for others to pass you easily.
Take great care where the Trans Pennine Trail crosses or follows roads.
Take all your litter home and be careful with cigarette ends due to risk of fire.
Dog owners please clean up after your pet - dog mess spoils the Trail.
Close control your dog, preferably on a short lead, especially around farm animals.

Horse Riders
Use only sections of the Trail where horses are allowed.
Do not use the Trail unless you can control your horse - you may encounter walkers, wheelchair and scooter users, cyclists, dogs and bridges over road, rail and water.
Do not canter or gallop on shared sections of the Trail.
Please avoid damaging Trail surfaces and don't ride on the grass central dividing strip.

Horse riders and cyclists
Warn others when you approach from behind so you do not startle people as you pass by - call politely or use a bell / hooter.
Slow down when approaching other users who are unpredictable, particularly children or animals; remember too, some people may have a hearing impairment.
Helmets / high visibility clothing add to your safety. Ride in single file on narrow sections.

Cyclists
Must not use this route for racing competitions or speed trials.
On canal towpaths - read and abide by the British Waterways code for cyclists.
Please be prepared to dismount occasionally - on steep access ramps, or on limited sections (such as restricted width bridges).
Where the Trail is a designated bridleway, cyclists should give way to other users.
Be careful with your speed - especially on slopes or where visibility ahead is limited.

Please enjoy the Trans Pennine Trail and help others to do so too!

Trail & Rail Planner
Showing rail stations near the trail

- Station
○ No station

Southport - Hornsea

- Southport
- Birkdale
- Hillside
- Ainsdale
- Old Roan
- Aintree
- Rice Lane / Orrell Park
- Broad Green
- Hunts Cross
- Halewood

- Runcorn
- Widnes
- Sankey for Penketh
- Warrington West
- Warrington Bank Quay
- Warrington Central
- Navigation Rd / Altrincham (1.5 miles)
- Trafford Park

- East Didsbury
- Stockport
- Brinnington
- Reddish South
- Hyde Central
- Godley
- Hattersley
- Broadbottom
- Hadfield / Glossop

- Penistone
- Silkstone Common North Option
- Elsecar South Option
- Wombwell
- Bolton Upon Dearne

- Conisbrough
- Doncaster
- Bentley
- Snaith

- Selby
- Howden
- Saltmarshe

- Broomfleet
- Brough
- Ferriby
- Hessle
- Hull
- Hornsea

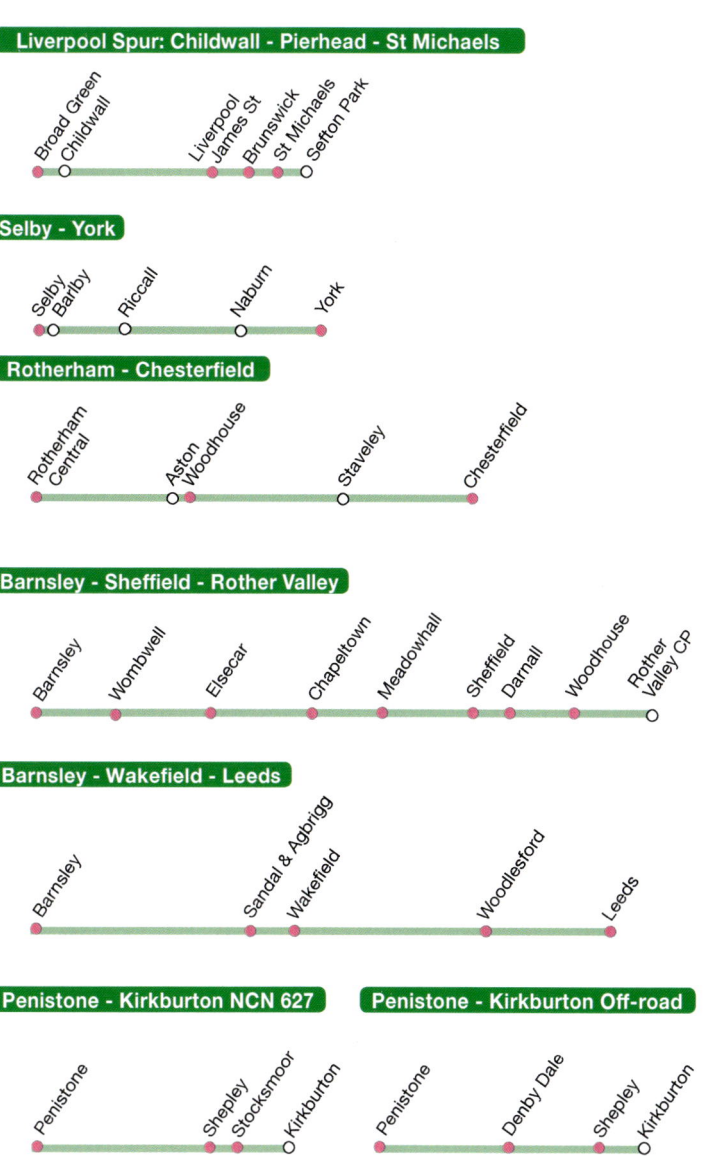

TPT GUIDE

Southport - Widnes

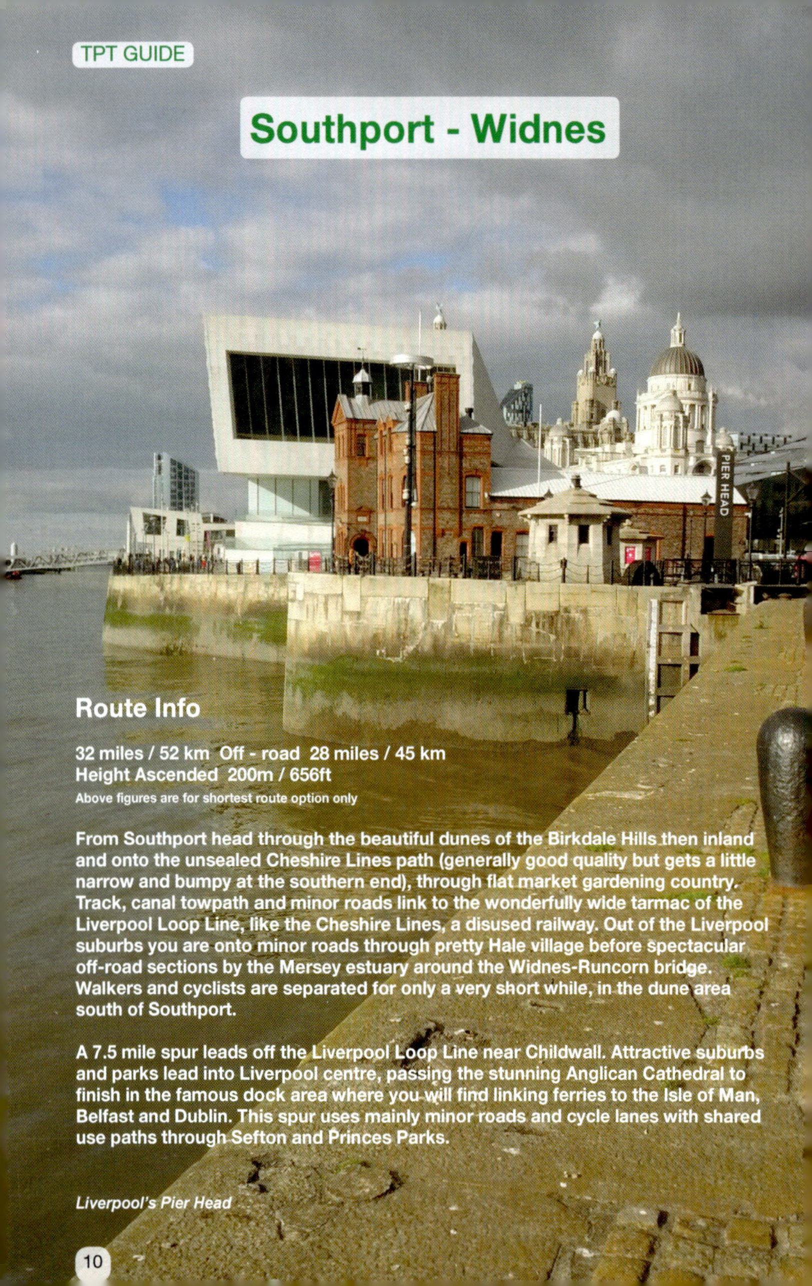

Route Info

32 miles / 52 km Off - road 28 miles / 45 km
Height Ascended 200m / 656ft

Above figures are for shortest route option only

From Southport head through the beautiful dunes of the Birkdale Hills then inland and onto the unsealed Cheshire Lines path (generally good quality but gets a little narrow and bumpy at the southern end), through flat market gardening country. Track, canal towpath and minor roads link to the wonderfully wide tarmac of the Liverpool Loop Line, like the Cheshire Lines, a disused railway. Out of the Liverpool suburbs you are onto minor roads through pretty Hale village before spectacular off-road sections by the Mersey estuary around the Widnes-Runcorn bridge. Walkers and cyclists are separated for only a very short while, in the dune area south of Southport.

A 7.5 mile spur leads off the Liverpool Loop Line near Childwall. Attractive suburbs and parks lead into Liverpool centre, passing the stunning Anglican Cathedral to finish in the famous dock area where you will find linking ferries to the Isle of Man, Belfast and Dublin. This spur uses mainly minor roads and cycle lanes with shared use paths through Sefton and Princes Parks.

Liverpool's Pier Head

TPT GUIDE

Don't Miss

- **Southport** is an elegant seaside town, with its grandest architecture, much of it Victorian and Edwardian, found along Lord St. Wandering the shopping arcades and pavement cafe sitting are favourite activities and the Wayfarers Arcade has to be one of the finest pieces of Victorian architecture in the country. Southport's attractive Marine Lake and Pier area, including the elegant Kings Gardens, front onto miles of open sand. The Pier is a particular attraction; it's the oldest in the UK and the second longest at over a kilometre. Temporarily closed for repairs at the time of writing.

If you are a fan of quirky attractions then look out for the outdoor Model Railway VIllage and the British Lawnmower Museum. Southport's Eco Centre houses a bike hire centre.

- The route passes by the **Birkdale and Ainsdale dunes,** an unusual landscape, the latter being a National Nature Reserve housing the Natterjack Toad and the Sand Lizard. The TPT walkers' route actually follows the Falklands Way through the dunes whilst the cyclists' route uses the pavement cycleway right next to them.

Lord Street, Southport

SOUTHPORT - WIDNES

Jubilee Bridge, Widnes

- A route option diverts off the Liverpool Loop Line to thread its way into Liverpool past some of its most iconic sights to arrive at the now transformed **Pier Head**. It is backed by the 'Three Graces' of the Royal Liver Building, the Cunard building and the Port of Liverpool Building. **Mersey Ferries** also depart from near here and now offer trips up the Manchester Ship Canal too (see pg34). The Isle of Man ferry departs from here too,

Just south of Pier Head is **Albert Dock**, now housing attractions including the Maritime Museum, Slavery Museum and Tate Liverpool. The waterway you see in front of the Three Graces is a link between the Leeds-Liverpool Canal and the South Docks. The £22 million 1.6 mile extension to the Leeds-Liverpool Canal was officially opened to boaters in 2009.

- The finale to your route passes under the graceful arch of the **Silver Jubilee Bridge** also known as the Runcorn Bridge. It opened in 1961 to replace the old transporter bridge whose old powerhouse is passed en route.

The Silver Jubliee Bridge has been redesigned as a local bridge now the new Mersey Gateway Bridge has been completed, with free access for locals and for cyclists and walkers.

- Just around a bend in the Mersey and under construction at the time of writing is the **Mersey Gateway Bridge,** an incredible feat of construction to link north and south of the Mersey with a six-lane cable-stayed bridge.

TPT GUIDE

❶ SOUTHPORT CYCLE HIRE
Eco Centre, Esplanade PR8 1RX
01704 500996 visitseftonandwestlancs.co.uk
Also a manned cycle hire outlet at Southport train station (summer weekdays only).

❷ MOSSCROP CYCLES
78 Bispham Road, PR9 7DF
01704 228805 mosscropcycles.co.uk

❸ POWERSTATION ELECTRIC BIKES
25 Kingsway, PR8 1ND 01704 510850
powerstation-ebikes.co.uk

❹ EVANS CYCLES
Ocean Plaza, Marine Drive PR8 1SB
0343 909 2707 evanscycles.com

❶ ANDYS CAFE Garrick Parade
Much-loved pie & chips establishment.
Amongst many others in Southport centre.

❶ NEW TALBOT HOTEL
23-25 Portland Street PR8 1LR
0758 1358039
thenewtalbot.co.uk

❷ THE PRINCE OF WALES HOTEL
Lord Street PR8 1JS
0871 2220039 britanniahotels.com

❸ TRAVELODGE
Garrick Parade, Lord Street PR8 1RN
08715 591862 travelodge.co.uk

❹ ROYAL CLIFTON HOTEL
The Promenade PR8 1RB
0871 222 1098 britanniahotels.com

❺ SOUTHPORT CENTRAL PREMIER INN
Marine Drive PR8 1RY
0871 5279012 premierinn.com

❻ THE VINCENT HOTEL
98 Lord Street PR8 1JR
01704 883 800 thevincenthotel.com

SOUTHPORT - WIDNES

Southport

⭐ *The Pier*
Over 1200 yards long it's the second longest in Great Britain. Closed for repair at time of writing.
⭐ *Kings Gardens* Victorian and Edwardian layout.
⭐ *Lord Street Shopping Arcades*
⭐ *Southport Pleasureland and Lakeside Miniature Railway*
Traditional and modern rides and attractiions.
⭐ *Southport Model Railway Village*
⭐ *Splash World*
Themed swimming pool with attractions such as water rides and the bubble spa.

7 SUNNYSIDE
47 Bath Street PR9 0DP
01704 536521 sunnysidesouthport.co.uk

8 LE MAITRE
69 Bath Street PR9 0DN
01704 530394 hotel-lemaitre.co.uk

9 THE LEICESTER HOTEL
24 Leicester Street PR9 0EZ
01704 530049 theleicester.com

10 EDENDALE HOUSE
83 Avondale Road North PR9 0NE
01704 530718 edendalehotel.co.uk

11 BOWDEN LODGE HOTEL
18 Albert Road PR9 0LE
01704 543531 bowdenlodge.co.uk

🔴 Route Notes   ⭐ See & Do   🔵 Sleep   ⛺ Campsite   🟢 Eat   ⚫ Cycle Shops   (with cafe)

15

SOUTHPORT - WIDNES

① Straight over crossroads onto Moor Lane.
② R off the road to follow Plex Moss Lane / North Moss Lane signs and L onto the Cheshire Lines path.

★ *Ainsdale Sand Dunes National Nature Reserve*
See Don't Miss pg12

★ *British Lawnmower Museum*
106-112 Shakespeare Street, Southport PR8 5AJ

① BIRKDALE GUEST HOUSE
87 Liverpool Road, Birkdale PR4 4DB
01704 551193

② N'ISTA BOUTIQUE ROOMS
41 Weld Road, Birkdale PR8 2DS
01704 808283 cafebarnista.co.uk

▲ LANDSDOWNE CAMPING
Shore Road, Hesketh Bank PR4 6XP
01772 814075 landsdownecamping.org.uk

▲ OLD MANOR FARM SITE
Shore Road, Hesketh Bank PR4 6XQ
07932 277025 old-manor-farm.co.uk

① HALFORDS
1 Kew Roundabout, Meols Cop Lane
Southport PR9 7RG

② MECYCLE
59 Station Road, Ainsdale PR8 3HH
01704 579353 autisminitiatives.org/mecycle
Open 8-8.

Lord Street, Southport

① Route Notes ★ See & Do ① Sleep ▲ Campsite ① Eat ① Cycle Shops (with cafe)

SOUTHPORT - WIDNES

1 At the end of the Cheshire Lines Path bear L and head across Sefton Lane onto Old Racecourse Road. R onto Meadway leads to a track across new woodland then a light controlled crossing of a main road at Brook House Lane.

2 Push up steps and ramp (steep) at Walleys Steps. R onto pavement cycle lane and in 650m R onto Heysham Road under rail tunnel. Immediate L onto path.

3 At track split head L past the back of Aintree train station. Emerge at main road - L here over rail bridge then R at main road junction. In 250m go L onto Melling Road and R onto Greenwich Road. At the first bridge access the Liverpool Loop Line and head L following NCN 62 signs to Walton Vale and West Derby.

1 THE STABLES INN LIVERPOOL AINTREE
1 Ormskirk Road, Aintree L9 5AS
0151 3081803   stablesinnaintree.co.uk

HIDDEN CORNER CAMPING
19 Millbank Lane, Maghull L31 9AT
0151 531 0688
campingandcaravanningclub.co.uk

1 LYDIATE
Running Horses (pub food) on Bell Lane, and also the Village Diner is a pleasant local cafe.

2 MAGHULL
Town centre has a wide selection of eateries and a supermarket.

1 HALFORDS
Unit 6 Racecourse Retail Park
Aintree Way, Aintree L9 5AN

2 HOBSON CYCLES
62 Walton Vale L9 2BU
0151 281 8941

3 SEFTON CYCLES
23 Dover Road, Maghull L31 5JB
0151 531 9849

Join the Livepool Loop Line at Aintree

1 Route Notes   ★ See & Do   **1** Sleep   Campsite   **1** Eat   **1** Cycle Shops   (with cafe)

SOUTHPORT - WIDNES

❶ Liverpool Spur Leave Liverpool Loop Line, following NCN 56 to Pier Head. The generally well-signed route uses suburban roads to climb over a steep hill at Childwall then heads towards Liverpool centre, passing Liverpool College and Greenbank Park and through Sefton and Princes Parks.

❷ Liverpool Spur A southern route option splits at Eros statue, Sefton Park. The main NCN 56 is signed, whilst the southern option is not. You need the second exit on the L from the main NCN56 exit. Signing becomes more apparent as you leave the park, heading onto Livingstone Drive North. It then uses suburban streets, passing St Michaels train station, before heading past the Festival Gardens and along the Mersey to Pier Head.

★ *Croxteth Hall and Country Park*
Hall, farm, walled garden, nature reserve, country park. (Hall temporarily closed)

★ *Calderstones Park*
The route passes right by this lovely 94 acre park with old English and Japanese gardens and a cafe. The Calderstones themselves are prehistoric, bear mysterious carvings and are preserved in their own glass structure.

★ *Sefton Park*
One of Liverpool's most famous parks, the highlight of its 235 acres undoubtedly being the magnificent Palm House.

❶ PREMIER INN LIVERPOOL WEST DERBY
Queens Drive, West Derby L13 0DL
0333 321 1231   premierinn.com

❷ TRAVELODGE LIVERPOOL STONEYCROFT
502 Queens Drive L13 0AS
08715 591827   travelodge.co.uk

❸ CHILDWALL ABBEY HOTEL
Childwall Abbey Road L16 5EY
0151 722 5293   childwallabbeyhotelpub.co.uk

LIVERPOOL SPUR

❹ SQUARE TREE HOUSE
Princes Park L8 3TZ
07976 610581

❺ GEORGIAN TOWN HOUSE HOTEL
60. UpperParliament Street L8 7LF
0151 708 0856
georgiantownhousehotel.co.uk

❻ BASE SERVICES APARTMENTS
2 Hudson Gardens, 136 Duke Street L1 5BB
0151 702 9222   baseservicedapartments.co.uk

❼ THE JOKER BOAT
Liverpool Marina, Coburg Wharf L3 4BP
thejokerboatliverpool.com

❶ CHILDWALL
Childwall Abbey pub before climbing Childwall Abbey Rd to Childwall Triangle where there is a row of shops including a delicatessen.

❷ CHINATOWN
Lots of restaurants around Nelson Street, easily spotted by its huge Chinese arch

❶ HOBSON CYCLES
62 Walton Vale L9 2BU
0151 281 8941

❷ OBAN CYCLES
59 Breck Road, Anfield L4 2QS 0151 263 6332
obancycles.net

❸ THE ROLLING FIX
196-8 Breck Road, Everton L5 6PX
0151 306 1398
therollingfix.co.uk

❹ HALFORDS
491 – 499 Edge Lane, Liverpool L13 1AA

❺ QUINN CYCLES
379 – 385 Edge Lane, Liverpool L7 9LQ
0151 228 6262
quinncycles.co.uk

❻ BERNARD BICYCLES LTD
260 Smithdown Road L15 5AH 07534 768299
bernardbicycles.co.uk

❼ BIKEOLOGY
319 Smithdown Road L15 0EB 0151 733 8799

At the time of writing Swedish company Voi were operating dockless e-scooter and e-bike hire in Liverpool - just get the Voi app for more details.

1 After descending Duke Street head R, onto pedestrianised, often very busy, Paradise Street

2 L onto Lord Street which joins motor traffic to climb and pass the statue of Queen Victoria at Derby Square. Descend James Street to Pier Head.

★ *Anglican Cathedral*
Gothic cathedral, the largest in Britain, designed by Giles Gilbert Scott. Begun in 1904 and completed in 1978! Largest working church organ in the world.

★ *Metropolitan Cathedral of Christ the King*
Iconic 1960s construction

★ *Pier Head*
See Don't Miss pg13

★ *Walker Art Gallery*
One of the largest English collections outside London

★ *Albert Dock & Museums*
See Don't Miss pg13

★ *Museum of Liverpool*
The first national museum devoted to the history of a regional city, built in 2011.

★ *Western Approaches*
The HQ of a major operational Royal Navy Command during WWII, the reinforced concrete bunker is now a war museum.

★ *St. John's Beacon Viewing Gallery*
450 ft high observation platform

SOUTHPORT - WIDNES

① AACHEN HOTEL
89-91 Mount Pleasant L3 5TB 0151 709 3477

② ADELPHI HOTEL
Ranelagh Street L3 5UL
0871 222 0029 britanniainn.com

③ PREMIER INN LIVERPOOL ONE
48 Hanover Street L1 4AF
0333 321 9282 premierinn.com

④ HILTON LIVERPOOL CITY CENTRE
3 Thomas Steers Way L1 8LW
0151 708 4200 hilton.com

⑤ PREMIER INN ALBERT DOCK
Britannia Building, Albert Dock L3 4AD
0333 321 1232 premierinn.com

⑥ YHA LIVERPOOL ALBERT DOCK
25 Tabley Street L1 8EE 0345 371 9527
yha.org.uk

⑦ TRAVELODGE LIVERPOOL CENTRAL
The Strand L2 0PP 08719 846486
travelodge.co.uk

⑧ PREMIER INN CITY CENTRE MOORFIELDS
Vernon Street L2 2AY 0333 321 1233
premierinn.com

❶ DECATHLON
18-20 Church Street L1 3AP 0151 245 6946
decathlon.co.uk

❷ GIANT STORE
29 Parliament Street L8 5RN 0151 707 6116
giant-liverpool.co.uk/gb

❶ Route Notes ★ See & Do ❶ Sleep Campsite Eat ❶ Cycle Shops (with cafe)   23

SOUTHPORT - WIDNES

1 Keep following signs for NCN 62 and Higher Rd through Halewood Triangle area.

2 Down Blackburn Drive enter Halewood Doorstep Green and head to the far end of the park and bear R, with the railway immediately on your L. Follow Speke Boulevard signs in this area.

3 Meet Speke Boulevard and follow the cycle lanes here until signs divert you under the road and L onto Clough Road.

4 L onto Hale Road and continue into Hale village

★ *Calderstones and Sefton Parks*
See pg 21.

★ *Speke Hall*
Fantastic 16th century Tudor manor house now owned by the National Trust.

1 PREMIER INN LIVERPOOL ROBY
Roby Road, Huyton L36 4HD
0333 321 1108 premierinn.com

2 ESKDALE B&B
2, Hillfoot Road, Hunts Cross L25 0NB
0151 486 2083 eskdalebandb.co.uk

3 TRAVELODGE JOHN LENNNON AIRPORT
1 Speke Hall Avenue, Speke L24 1UX
08719 846528 travelodge.co.uk

4 PREMIER INN LIVERPOOL JOHN LENNON AIRPORT
57 Speke Hall Avenue, Speke L24 1YQ
0333 321 1235 premierinn.com

5 GATEWAY LODGE
1 Speke Church Road, Speke L24 3TA
0151 284 4801 gatewaylodgeuk.com

1 THE TURNPIKE
Bowring Park Road. Pub restaurant running from breakfast to evening.

2 Morrisons cafe, Subway sandwiches etc in The Speke Centre (shopping centre).

Statue of John Middleton at Hale (overleaf)

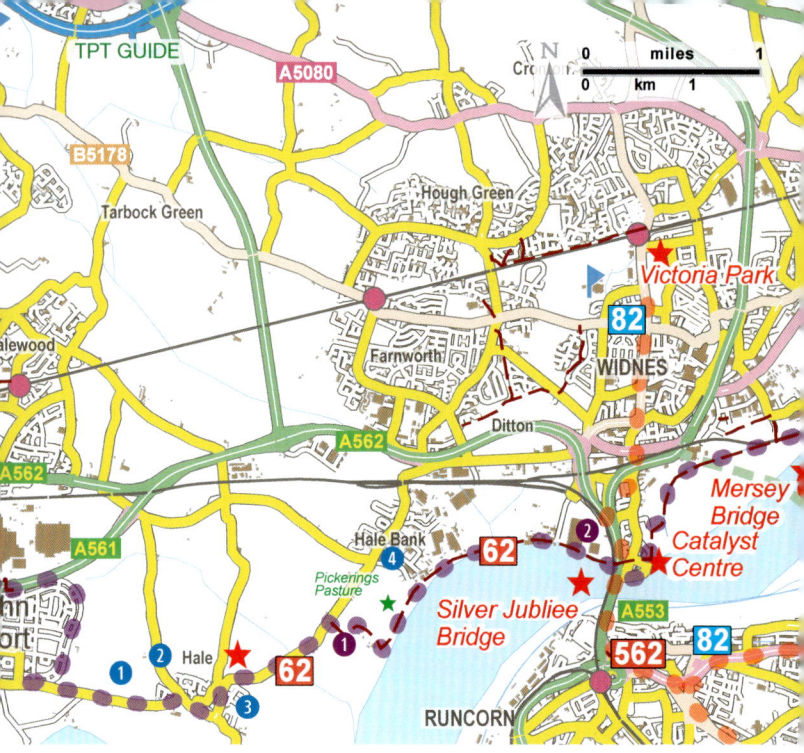

① R onto water treatment works access road then L through woods to Pickerings Pasture. Follow Merseyside path to cross over the bridge and up the ramp-steps at Dittons Brook and under the rail and Jubilee Bridges onto Parsonage Road.

② **Link to Widnes centre** Between the rail and Silver Jubilee Bridge head L up the west side of Jubilee Bridge and under it onto Cholmondeley St. R onto Irwell St then follow map opposite.

★ *Hale* Pretty village with unusual statue of John Middleton (the Childe of Hale) in front of the attractive Manor House. Reputed to have been 9feet 3inches tall, he is buried in the churchyard. There is a lighthouse a short walk from the village on the coast at Hale Head

★ *Bridges across the Mersey*
See Don't Miss pg13

★ *Victoria Park, Widnes* 🍴
Butterfly House and glasshouse amongst other features in this grand park. Several attractive refreshment opportunities.

★ *Catalyst Science Discovery Centre* 🍴
See pg32

① BROOK BARN B&B
Brookfarm, 66 Hale Road, Hale Village L24 5RF
07714 107 449
brookbarnbandb.co.uk

② THE BARN B & B
Ramsbrook Lane, Hale Village L24 5RP
0151 425 2781 / 07815 193003
barnbandb.com

SOUTHPORT - WIDNES

❸ CHURCH END FARMHOUSE
5 Church End Hale Village L24 4AX
0151 425 4273   churchendfarm.co.uk

❹ THE MERSEYVIEW HOTEL (PUB)
2 Mersey View Road WA8 8LP   07542 400223
merseyviewpubhotel.co.uk

❺ PREMIER INN WIDNES HOTEL
Venture Fields, Widnes WA8 0GY
0333 321 9239   premierinn.com

❻ TRAVELODGE WIDNES
Fiddlers Ferry Road A562 Widnes WA8 0HA
08719 846183   travelodge.co.uk
Runcorn across the bridge has accommodation.

❶ JOHN GEDDES CYCLES
43 Widnes Road, Widnes WA8 6AZ
0151 4207797 / 07511 227291
johngeddes.co.uk

 Route Notes   See & Do   Sleep   Campsite   Eat   Cycle Shops   (with cafe)

27

TPT GUIDE

Widnes - Stockport

Route Info

32miles / 51km
Off-road 25 miles / 40km
Height Ascended 277m / 909ft
Above figures are for shortest route option only

At Widnes you pick up the good quality St. Helens Canal towpath with fine views over the Mersey Estuary. Crossing the Mersey south of Warrington leads to a short section alongside the Manchester Ship Canal. A 9 mile / 15km section of disused railpath then crosses the Cheshire plain and enters the Trafford district of Greater Manchester.
Although this area is often associated with chemical production the trail largely avoids areas of heavy industry and passes close to the rural gem of Grappenhall and very pretty Lymm.

Along the Mersey Valley, south of Manchester the route uses a wide-ranging mixture of paths (mountain bike or touring tyres recommended) before approaching Didsbury village.
Finally you approach Stockport (a gem of attractive Victorian buildings with a beautiful old market hall) along a nice section of path by the river Mersey. There are several walkers' options approaching Stockport.
Signage is generally good, eased by the fact you are following NCN 62 all the way. Unfortunately the sections between Thelwall and Altrincham and Stretford and Stockport have a number of access barriers that may be tricky to negotiate with trailers and tandems or other heavy or unusually sized bikes. Tracks are generally unsealed though broad, with occasional narrower sections.

Beside the River Mersey

TPT GUIDE

Don't Miss

- Historic **Grappenhall and Lymm** villages are short detours off the route and Lymm in particular has plenty of attractive looking eating options.

Both are situated on the attractive Bridgewater Canal. Grappenhall's small centre is based around a cobbled square with a church and two ancient pubs whilst Lymm is much larger. Its centre encompasses a central conservation area including an ancient cross whose original purpose remains lost in time (the modern extension on top is Victorian). The town cryer still uses it for proclamations! Other Lymm attractions include the Victorian dam bordered by ancient woodland. Another hidden corner is the Slitting Mill and gorge (used for metalworking).

- **The Mersey reborn;** despite being associated with heavy industry and its legacy of pollution in recent centuries and decades the river Mersey is now starting a rebirth and it accompanies you for much of the way on this section. In particular look out for the viewing platform just past the Mersey Gateway bridge as a great wildlife viewing spot. Expect to see cormorants and kingfishers amongst much else. The trail links wildlife spots such as Dainewell Woods, Kickety Brook and Chorlton Ees, also home to a wealth of flora and fauna.

Simon's Bridge over the Mersey near Didsbury shows how nature is recolonising a once polluted river

WIDNES - STOCKPORT

Stockport's historic centre

- **Dunham Massey** is a fine Georgian stately home surrounded by a magnificent Deer Park. Although you need to pay an entrance fee to look at the house there is a public footpath across the rear of it (see map on page 35 for road detour to main access and path).

On a visit to the house you will discover fine collections of silver and furniture. The house itself is moated and surrounded by formal gardens (including a huge Winter Garden) and there are also stables and a carriage house. The grounds feature a working saw mill.

- **Stockport Centre** houses a lovely Victorian market and Produce Hall and nearby church, plus a fine collection of older buildings such as Underbank House, Staircase House and the dizzying changes in street level make it a great place for walking around. The magnificent Plaza is a 1930s theatre and film venue totally restored in the original style.

Other sights and attractions include the 111 foot high viaduct bestriding the town, the Hat Works Museum (the UK's only dedicated hat museum) and Stockport Air Raid Shelters (a network almost a mile long built to protect local inhabitants during WWII and capable of housing several thousand).

① Head along a combination of backstreets and estuaryside paths, and around the Spike Island area to join the St Helen's Canal towpath.

② Leave St Helens canal towpath to follow signs through Arpley Meadows then just under rail bridges L onto towpath by disused canal.

③ Follow signs L then R across Chester Road then at canal basin split L and L onto Greenhalls Av. R on meeting London Rd and L onto path alongside Ship Canal.

④ Head across B5157 to a path leads to Clearwater Quays and a roundabout where you go R onto Thelwall Lane. Head over the impressive Latchford Locks.

⑤ Over Latchford Locks R then immediate L onto Bradshaw Lane. Shortly L onto railpath.

★ *Mersey Bridges*
See Don't Miss entry in previous chapter pg 13

★ *Catalyst Science Discovery Centre* 🍽
Interactive science centre and museum. Shop and cafe and glass lift to rooftop observatory.

🔵① VICTORIA LODGE
5 Victoria Road, Stockton Heath WA4 2AL
01925 263060 victorialodgestocktonheath.com

🟢① FERRY TAVERN Great drinks selection and hot pies as a bar snack

🟢② STOCKTON HEATH Many trendy eateries

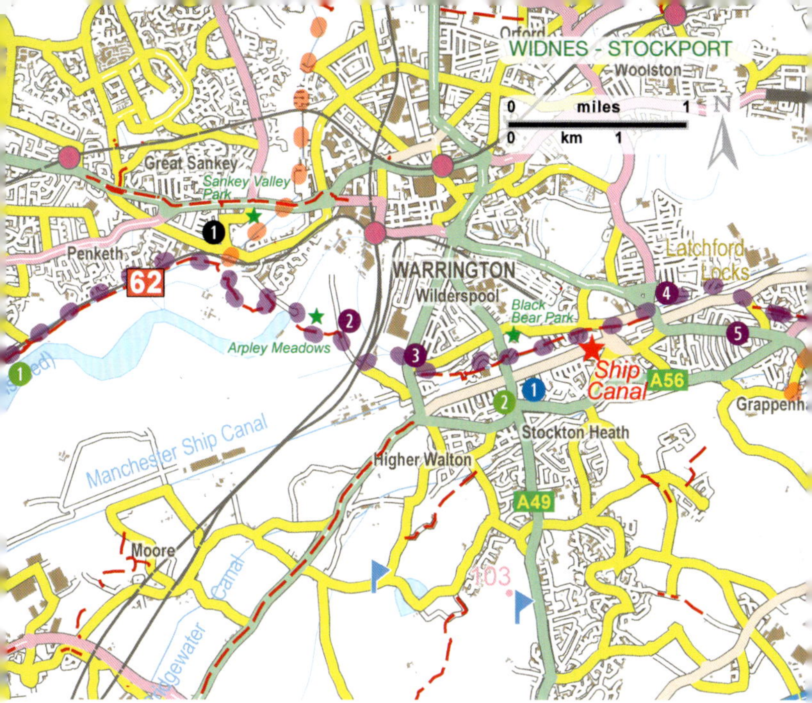

WIDNES - STOCKPORT

① D & M CYCLES
2 Hood Lane, Sankey WA5 1EJ
01925 653606
dandmcycles.com

⭐ *Manchester Ship Canal*
The largest river navigation canal in the world when it opened in 1894. Although little used these days you can admire this immense feat of engineering on organised cruises run by Mersey Ferries (Liverpool Pier Head to Salford Quays).

St Helens Canal

 Route Notes ⭐ See & Do   Sleep   Campsite   Eat   Cycle Shops (with cafe)

① Trail option To detour to Grappenhall exit the trail on the R marked Bridgewater Canal (VERY narrow access point to negotiate). Walkers can use the canal towpath as a direct link to the village but cyclists must use the road link via Halfacre La, Weaste La, Cliff La and Bellhouse La.

★ *Grappenhall & Lymm*
See Don't Miss page 30

★ *Dunham Massey*
See Don't Miss page 31

★ *Denzell Gardens*
Attractive 19th century house in public parkland

① STATHAM LODGE HOTEL
Warrington Road, Lymm WA13 9BP
01925 752204   stathamlodge.com

② ASH FARM COUNTRY GUEST HOUSE
Park Lane, Little Bollington WA14 4TJ
0161 929 9290 / 0754 220 3995   ashfarm.co.uk

③ THE OLD POST OFFICE
Park Lane, Little Bollington WA14 4TQ
01565 746600   cheshirebreaks.com

④ TRAVELODGE ALTRINCHAM CENTRAL
Grafton Tower, Stamford New Road,
Altrincham WA14 1SB
08719 846509   travelodge.co.uk

⑤ PREMIER INN MANCHESTER ALTRINCHAM HOTEL
Manchester Road, Altrincham WA14 4PH
0333 321 1306   premierinn.com

⑥ BEST WESTERN CRESTA COURT HOTEL
Church Street, Altrincham WA14 4DP
0161 927 7272
cresta-court.co.uk

HOLLYBANK PARK
Warburton Bridge Road, Rixton WA3 6HU
0161 210 2524   caravanparkscheshire.co.uk

① GRAPPENHALL
Parr Arms, Rams Head and Bellhouse pubs.

② LYMM has a wide range of cafes and restaurants, including several continental choices

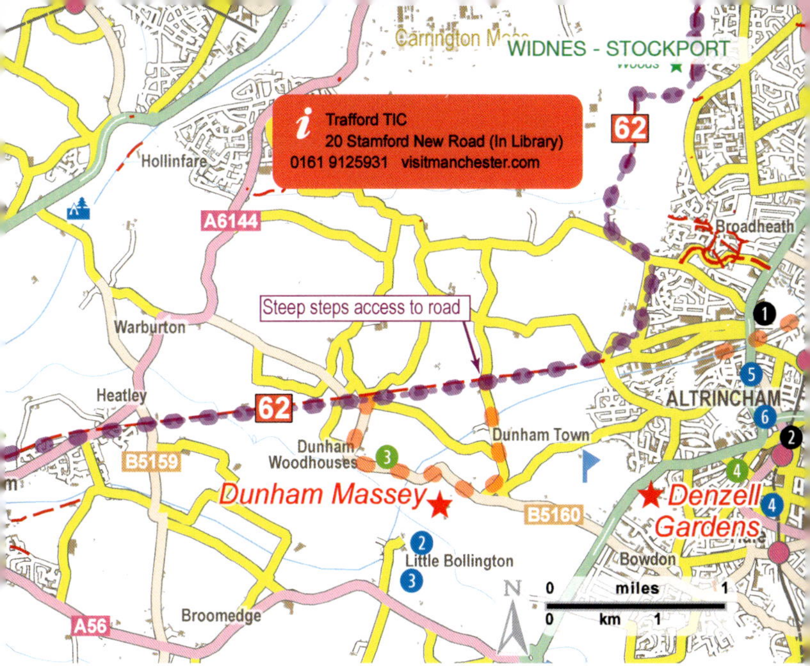

WIDNES - STOCKPORT

Trafford TIC
20 Stamford New Road (In Library)
0161 9125931   visitmanchester.com

3 If you opt for the unsigned road loop via Dunham Massey you have the choice of the Rope & Anchor pub, Dunham Massey Ice Cream shop, the cafe at Dunham Massey house, tea room at Dunham Barn or the Axe & Cleaver Pub.

4 ALTRINCHAM
Short ride from the trail at Dairyhouse Lane, housing a beautifully restored market that has a great concentration of upmarket eateries, including a modern take on black pudding! Next door is a fine outdoor market if you want to stock up on basics for the panniers.

1 HALFORDS
Unit 1 Manchester Road
Broadheath Altrincham WA14 5PZ

2 Also around Altrincham are:
HALE CYCLEWORKS
38 Stamford Park, Altrincham WA15 9EW
0161 928 6549   halecycleworks.co.uk
STAMFORD CYCLE COMPANY
5 Moss Lane, Altrincham WA14 1BA
07512 526631   stamfordcycleco.co.uk

Dunham Massey - a short detour from the TPT

● Route Notes   ★ See & Do   ● Sleep   ⛺ Campsite   ● Eat   ● Cycle Shops   (with cafe)

① A light controlled crossing takes you across busy Carrington Lane onto quieter Banky Lane. At the end of it R, leading to a traffic-free path.

② Pass alongside Hawthorn Road and under the Bridgewater Canal, passing an attractive church.

③ **Trail option** Having gone down a sliproad off the A5103 (bus lane and cycle lane only) pass under the M60 and for a pleasant traffic-free route immediate L into the woods (there is a route option straight on via Northenden).

④ Past Didsbury golf course the cycle option crosses the river (walking option rejoins route here) and split L, away from the river past the sports ground. Quiet Ford Lane brings you to a main road from where the route is well signed on roads through Didsbury.

⑤ Out of Didsbury route crosses and follows tram tracks.

⑥ Leave the tram tracks to cross the A5145, then in 250m bear R off the cycle path, descending to eventually join the Mersey and head L. You then parallel the river on your R, to the 'Pyramid' building on the edge of Stockport. Map overleaf for Stockport route options.

★ *Sale Water Park* 🍴
152 acres of countryside around an artificial lake with several eating options

★ *Wythenshawe Hall* 🍴
Ancestral home of the Tatton family. Surrounded by beautiful parkland with cafe.

★ *Fletcher Moss Park & Parsonage Gardens and nearby Didsbury Park* 🍴
Fletcher Moss has gardens, meadow and woodland and, like nearby Didsbury Park, has a cafe

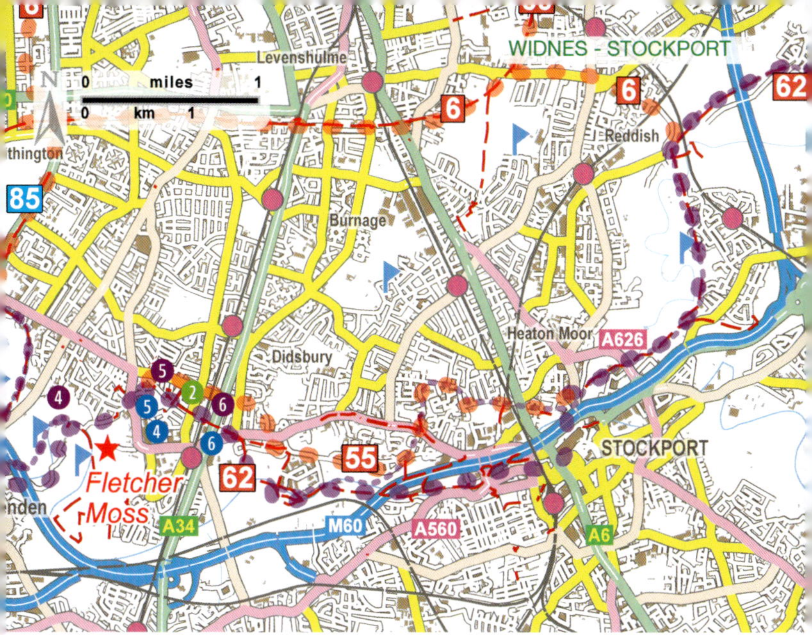

① **PREMIER INN MANCHESTER SALE**
Carrington Lane, Ashton-Upon-Mersey,
Sale M33 5BL
0333 321 1295   premierinn.com

② **PREMIER INN MANCHESTER WEST DIDSBURY HOTEL**
Christie Fields Business Park
Derwent Avenue, West Didsbury M21 7QS
0333 321 1298   premierinn.com

③ **BRITANNIA COUNTRY HOUSE HOTEL**
Palatine Road, Didsbury M20 2WG
0871 222 0016   britanniahotels.com

④ **DIDSBURY HOUSE HOTEL**
Didsbury Park, Didsbury Village M20 5LJ
0161 448 2200   didsburyhouse.co.uk

⑤ **ELEVEN DIDSBURY PARK**
Didsbury Park, Didsbury Village M20 5LH
0161 448 7711   elevendidsburypark.co.uk

⑥ **TRAVELODGE MANCHESTER DIDSBURY**
Parrs Wood Centre, Wilmslow Road
Off A34 Kingsway, East Didsbury M20 5PG
08719 846162   travelodge.co.uk

① **JACKSON'S BOAT**, Jackson's Bridge Nice location, pub food. Also nearby is Sale Water Park with three eateries. Access from the TPT via Jackson's Bridge past Jackson's Boat pub

② **DIDSBURY** has plenty of cafes near route

① **DEVEREUX CYCLES**
45 Green Lane, Sale M33 5PN   0161 973 5234
devereuxcycles.com

② **KEN FOSTERS CYCLE LOGIC**
374 – 376 Barlow Moor Road
Chorlton-cum-Hardy M21 8AZ   0161 881 7160
kenfosterscyclelogic.co.uk

③ **VELO TIMES**
Rifle Rd, Jacksons Bridge M33 2LX
0161 258 8434   Hire & repairs
velotimes.com

④ **A1 CYCLE CENTRE (ROCHE SPARES)**
414 – 416 Palatine Road, Northenden M22 4JT
0161 998 2882

 Route Notes   See & Do   Sleep   Campsite   Eat   Cycle Shops   (with cafe)

❶ Trail option Kings Reach bridleway ends at the route junction by the 'Pyramid' Coop building on a bridge. There are two options here - follow the river path ahead (which involves climbing shallow steps and heading over the river), or heading R across the bridge and L onto Brinksway, crossing a busy junction.

★ *Spiral Ramps*
£1 billion scheme to to transform Stockport Interchange has created spiral cycle access ramps overhanging the Mersey and a rooftop garden

★ *Underbank Hall*
16th Century town house with wonderful facade. Now a bank.

★ *Staircase House*
Stockport's most ancient house, now a museum.

★ *Hat Works Museum*
Details of one of the town's once most important industries.

★ *Plaza Cinema & Theatre*
Wonderful Art Deco facade and sumptuous interior.

★ *Air Raid Shelters*
Carved out of solid rock during WWII and able to house several thousand people.

① **HOLIDAY INN EXPRESS STOCKPORT**
11 Station Road. Stockport SK3 9JD
0161 3596363   ihg.com

② **THE RED BULL**
14 Middle Hillgate, Stockport SK1 3AY
0161 480 1286   robinsonsbrewery.com

③ **PREMIER INN STOCKPORT CENTRAL**
48 Churchgate, Stockport SK1 1YG
0333 321 9032   premierinn.com

① **DECATHLON**
Georges Road SK4 1DN
0161 4769600   decathlon.co.uk

② **WILLS WHEELS**
482 Manchester Road SK4 5DL 0161 432 4936
willswheelsshop.co.uk

③ **WOODSONS CYCLES**
85c Castle Street. Edgeley SK3 9AR
0161 480 8725   woodsoncycles.co.uk

④ **HALFORDS**
2 Manchester Road SK4 1TN

⑤ **EVANS CYCLES**
Unit 2, The Courts SK1 1UD
0343 909 2741   evanscycles.com

Ⓜ **M60 MOBILE CYCLE REPAIRS**
07747 838580   m60mcr.co.uk
cover the TPT from about Altrincham to Hyde.

Route Notes ★ See & Do Sleep Campsite Eat Cycle Shops (with cafe)

39

TPT GUIDE

Stockport - Penistone

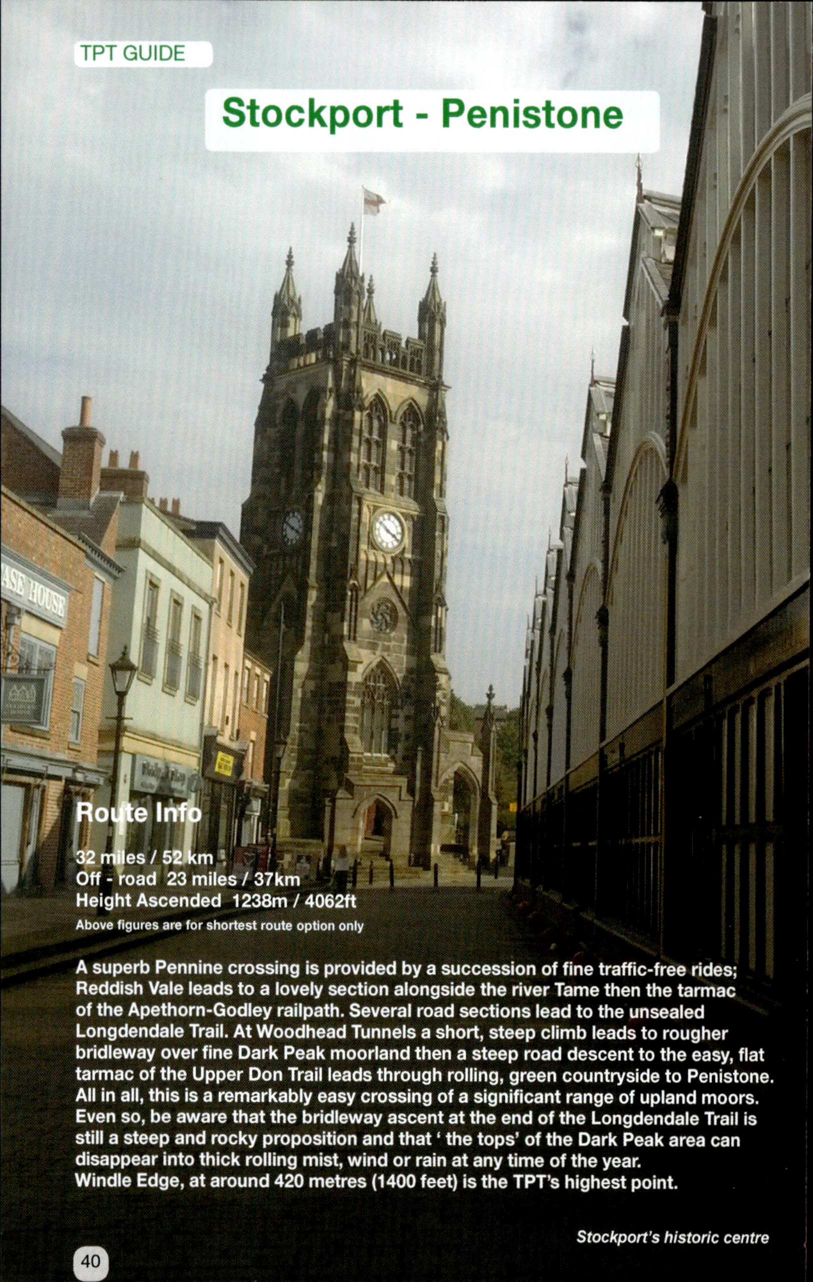

Route Info

32 miles / 52 km
Off - road 23 miles / 37km
Height Ascended 1238m / 4062ft

Above figures are for shortest route option only

A superb Pennine crossing is provided by a succession of fine traffic-free rides; Reddish Vale leads to a lovely section alongside the river Tame then the tarmac of the Apethorn-Godley railpath. Several road sections lead to the unsealed Longdendale Trail. At Woodhead Tunnels a short, steep climb leads to rougher bridleway over fine Dark Peak moorland then a steep road descent to the easy, flat tarmac of the Upper Don Trail leads through rolling, green countryside to Penistone. All in all, this is a remarkably easy crossing of a significant range of upland moors. Even so, be aware that the bridleway ascent at the end of the Longdendale Trail is still a steep and rocky proposition and that ' the tops' of the Dark Peak area can disappear into thick rolling mist, wind or rain at any time of the year.
Windle Edge, at around 420 metres (1400 feet) is the TPT's highest point.

Stockport's historic centre

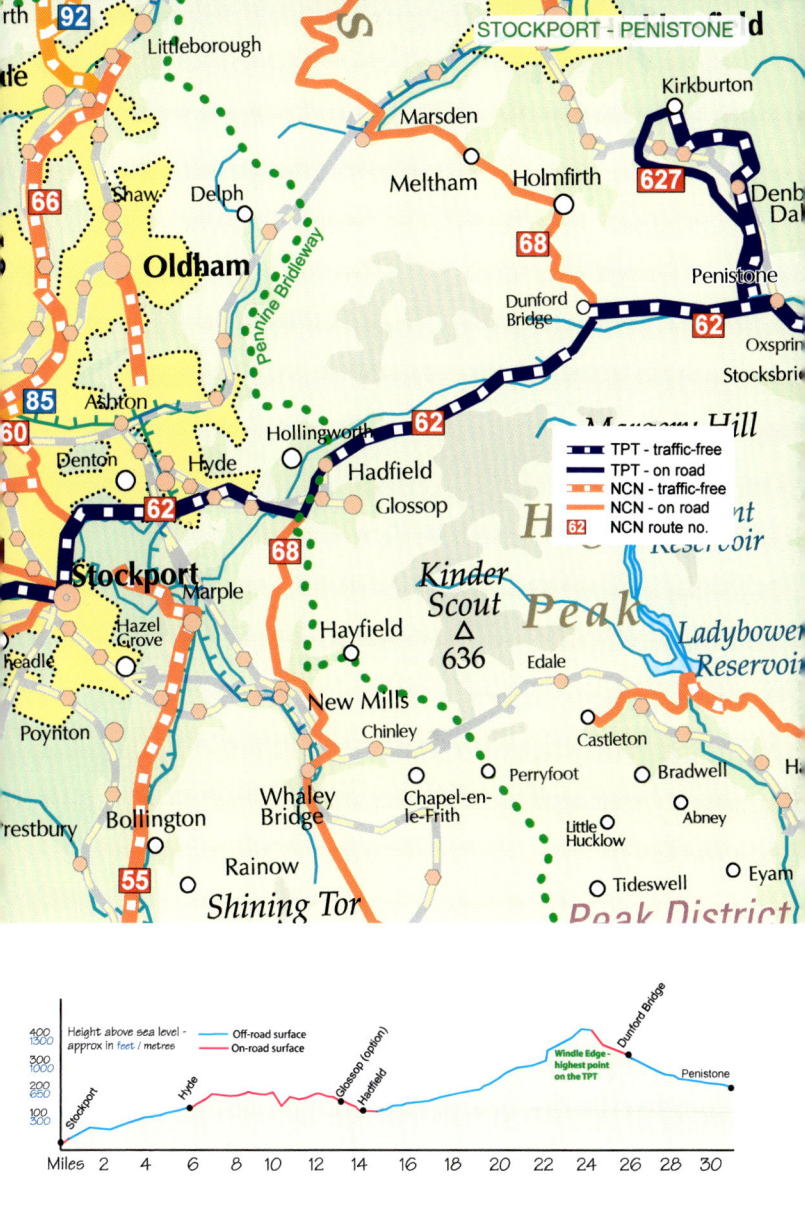

TPT GUIDE

Reddish Vale Country Park

Don't Miss

• **Reddish Vale Country Park** is on the edge of Stockport with cycle trails, nature trails, bridleways, a local nature reserve, butterfly conservation park and woodlands. The trail passes right by the visitor centre where there is a lovely lake which has a 17 arched viaduct as a spectacular backdrop. reddishvalecountrypark.com
Leaving Reddish Vale up a track and coming into Denton you pass the 17th century brick facade of Hyde Hall, whose somewhat dilapidated appearance belies a long history, including a visit from Queen Anne (the British Queen who had seventeen pregnancies but no surviving children).

• **Broad Mills Heritage Site** is right on the eastern end of the walking option that passes over Werneth Low Country Park and only a couple of minutes from the cycling and walking options. Once the site of three large cotton spinning mills on the River Etherow, these are now long gone, leaving only picturesque stone ruins in this exquisite river valley. You can stock up on tasty treats at nearby Lymefield Garden Centre and choose your spot for a picnic in this idyllic river valley setting.

• Tiny **Tintwistle** village centre is just off the eastern route option leaving Hadfield.
If you navigate across the horrible traffic of the A628 to the northern part of the village you will find a lovely little village centre with some buildings dating as far back the 16th century. Pride of place must go to the ancient Bulls Head with a grand interior that must be seen!

STOCKPORT - PENISTONE

- **Glossop** is not directly on the TPT but makes a great detour (see suggested route detour pgs 46-49) Two towns in one, with the main town centre an impressive collection of Victorian buildings and the Old Town having a 17th century village feel with cobbled streets. Beautiful parks and plentiful accommodation mean this is a good overnight option too.
- **Penistone** is a fine Pennine market town set amidst glorious scenery. 13th century church and 18th century Cloth Hall and Shambles. It even has its own cinema and a deli cafe by the church.
- **Fine railpaths.** On this section you will encounter two of the best surfaced railpaths you will find anywhere in the UK

The Apethorne-Godley railpath is a great example of an urban railpath built to a high quality, whilst Dunford Bridge to Penistone passes through magnificent Pennine scenery.

The Upper Don trail has a fine tarmac surface and stunning views over the surrounding Pennine hills.

Penistone town centre

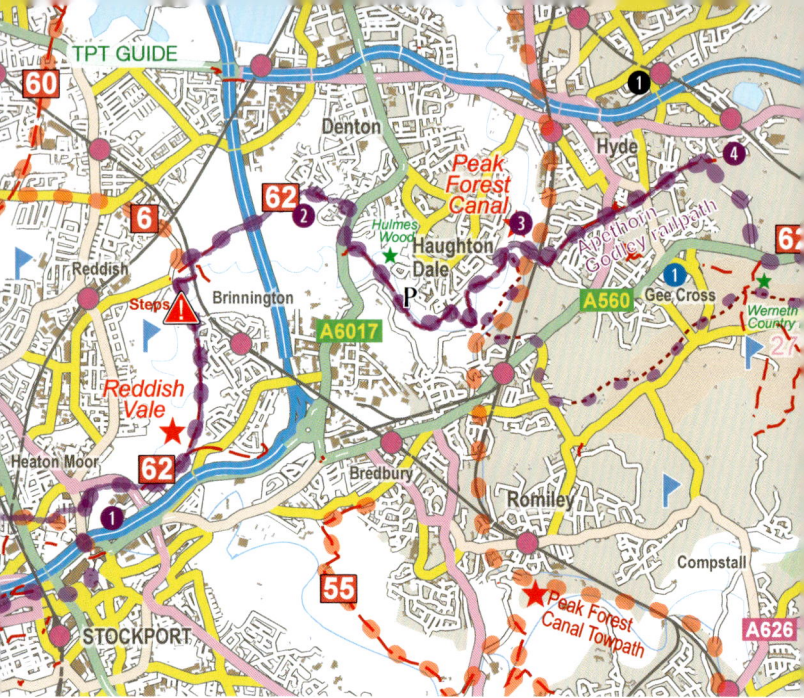

1 See town map on pages 38-39 for route out of Stockport centre. Up Lancashire Hill turn R onto Penny Lane then almost immediately R to descend through woods and bear L onto a path through Reddish Vale, with the river Tame on your R.

2 Easy to Miss! Turn R off Kingsley Close in Denton. The off-road link emerges at Yew Tree Rd. Turn L onto it.

3 Cycling and walking route crosses Gibraltar Bridge then shortly joins the Apethorn to Godley railpath by turning off White Terrace . At Gibraltar Bridge walking route heads up remarkable cobbled lane through woods to join the Peak Forest Canal.

4 Easy to Miss! Exit the railpath at a bridge to bear L onto bumpy farm track (Green Lane) leading up to the A560. Look out for NCN62 signs.

5 R off A560 up Clough End Rd and immediate L onto Broadbent Grove where trail is joined on the R.

6 Easy to Miss! Exiting Broadbottom La through Hurst Clough take an immediate R to exit Winslow Av. and R onto Broadbottom Rd.

7 Route Option for Glossop at Charlesworth (via Simmondley). Head straight over at the crossroads, not L on the TPT. This unsigned route is hilly with some motor traffic, but very scenic and avoids the less scenic area of Gamesley. See map pgs 46-49.

STOCKPORT - PENISTONE

⭐ *Reddish Vale Country Park*
See Don't Miss

⭐ *Peak Forest Canal*
Lovely narrow canal used by the Werneth Low walking route option.

⭐ *Werneth Low Country Park*
Stunning views, daytime or evening, over Greater Manchester and the Peak District and even as far as the Welsh hills. Dramatically sited war memorial

⭐ *Broad Mills Heritage Site*
See Don't Miss pg 42.

1 THE BUXTON INN
34 – 36 Mottram Old Road
Gee Cross Hyde SK14 5NG
0161 366 1534   thebuxtoninn.co.uk

2 PREMIER INN MANCHESTER HYDE
Stockport Road, Mottram, Hyde SK14 3AU
0333 321 1293   premierinn.com

⛺ ELIZABETH COTTAGE CAMPING
Park Cottage, Woodseats Lane, Charlesworth
SK13 5DR   07974 364470

1 HARE & HOUNDS, Werneth Low.
Great viewpoints and good food on the walking route.

2 LYMEFIELD GARDEN CENTRE
Atractive cafe with high quality food and a food shop.

3 CHARLESWORTH
Several opportunities including takeaway fish & chips at the George and Dragon pub food, Bake & Muffin Cafe on Marple Road and Village Greens grocer.

1 THE BIKE SHACK
4 Commercial Brow, Hyde SK14 2JW
0161 368 0906

M NEVER MIND THE BIKESHOPS
Mobile repair service
07940 859672   nevermindthebikeshops.com

 Route Notes   See & Do   Sleep   Campsite   Eat   Cycle Shops (with cafe)

TPT GUIDE

1 **Trail option** at roundabout by New Lamp pub. L down Waterside for the more scenic option across the foot of the dam, on a path off Goddard Lane near Tintwistle, or R up Station Road for the less scenic but easier road route through Hadfield (join trail just past rail station).

2 The Longdendale trail ends as it emerges into a former car parking area; the trail hairpins back up the hill to cross the busy A626. Care required!

3 Climb steeply up the rocky slope and join a better, more level track across the moor, bearing R onto it.

★ *Melandra Roman Fort*
Ancient monument accessible on foot from the TPT.

★ *Longdendale Valley.*
Houses the TPT's Longdendale Trail and a string of impressive reservoirs. Located in the Dark Peak area of the Peak National Park, just north of the forbidding, peaty mass of Bleaklow. Dramatic views down the valley over Woodhead Reservoir as you climb to Windle Edge, highest

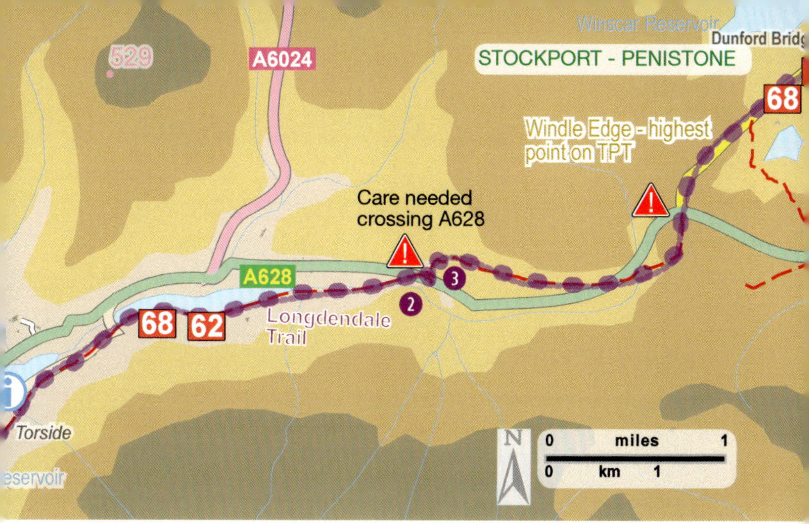

point on the TPT. Middle Black Clough waterfall is about a 20 min walk from the car park by the Trail near where it crosses the A628 Woodhead Road before you start up the hill - see peakdistrictwalks.net/middle-black-clough.waterfall-walk/

① WINDY HARBOUR FARM HOTEL
Woodhead Road, Glossop SK13 7QE
01457 853107 windyharbour.co.uk
▲ also.

② WHITE HOUSE FARM
147 Padfield Main Road, Padfield SK13 1ET
01457 854695
thepennineway.co.uk/whitehousefarm/

CROWDEN FARM CCC CAMPSITE
Crowden, Woodhead Road SK13 1HZ
01457 866057 campingandcaravanningclub.co.uk

① BULLS HEAD Tintwistle
An incredible interior with well-received pub food. Just off the trail in Tintwistle old centre.

② TORSIDE CAR PARK Mobile catering at times

For Glossop accommodation see overleaf.

The Longdendale Trail

① Route Notes   ★ See & Do   ① Sleep   ▲ Campsite   ① Eat   ① Cycle Shops   (with cafe)

47

TPT GUIDE

Glossop

★ New Glossop
'New' Glossop (19th century is new in this context) is visited on this alternative route, now a thriving former cotton and calico town blending wonderfully solid and impressive traditional archtecture with a modern influx of attractive cafes and restaurants. Of the many fine buildings hightlights are:

★ Market Hall
Undergoing renovation at time of writing

★ Partington Theatre
The local theatre company presents regular plays

★ Old Glossop
'Old' Glossop is a conservation area just to the north-east of lovely Manor Park (miniature railway in the summer), featuring old weavers cottages, a medieval market cross and some fine old pubs.

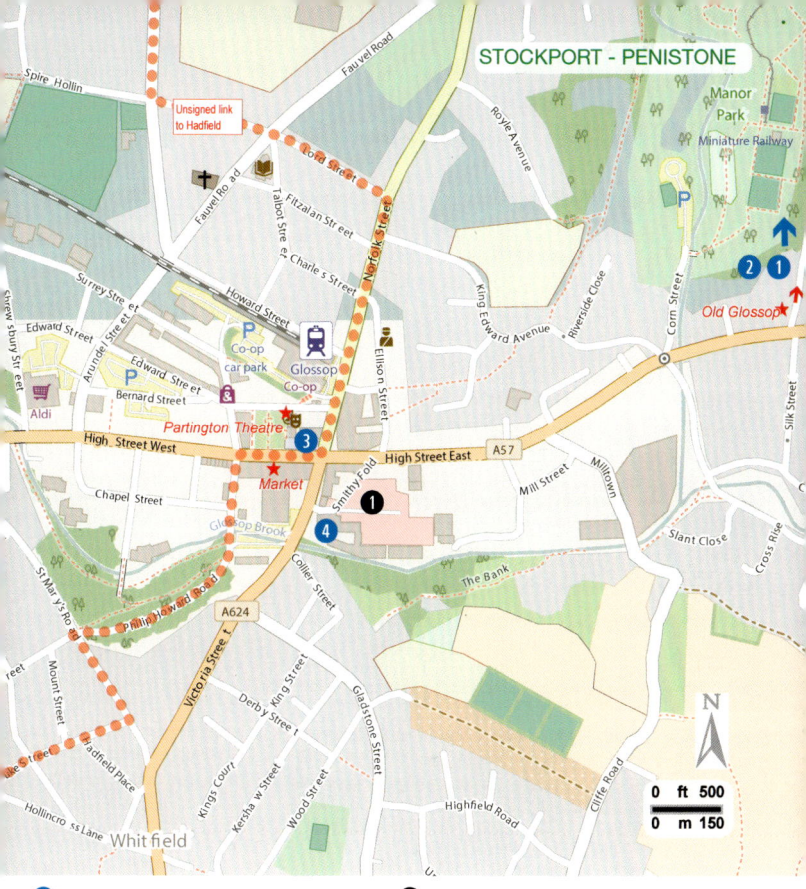

STOCKPORT - PENISTONE

① **BULLS HEAD**
102 Church St, Glossop, SK13 7RN
01457 855228 bullsheadglossop.com

② **QUEENS ARMS**
1 Shepley Street, Old Glossop SK13 7RZ
01457 853005 queensarmsglossop.co.uk

③ **NORFOLK ARMS INN**
Norfolk St, SK13 8BP
01457 851940
joseph-holt.com/pubs/norfolk-arms

④ **TRAVELODGE**
Victoria Street SK13 8HT
0871 9846330 travelodge.co.uk

❶ **HIGH PEAK CYCLES**
2 Smithy Fold, Glossop SK13 8DD
01457 861535 high-peak-cycles.com

❶ Route Notes ★ See & Do ① Sleep ⛺ Campsite ● Eat ● Cycle Shops ☕ (with cafe)

1 DOG & PARTRIDGE INN
Bordhill, Flouch S36 4HH
01226 763173   dogandpartridgeinn.co.uk

2 MILLBROOK B&B
Millhouse Lane , Millhouse Green S36 9NU
07792 105067   millbrook-bb.co.uk

3 BLACKSMITHS ARMS
Manchester Road, Millhouse Green S36 9NQ
01226 763485

THURLMOOR FARM CCC SITE
Carlecotes , Dunford Bridge S36 4TD
01226 762681   thurlmoor.site
No toilets or showers

WOODLAND VIEW CCC SITE
322 Barnsley Road, Hoylandswaine
Penistone S36 7HA
01226 761906   campingandcaravanningclub.co.uk

HOODLANDS FARM CAMPSITE
Fulshaw Lane, Penistone S36 9FD
07557 685678
hoodlandsfarmcampsite.business.site

1 MAGIC WOOD CAFE Hazlehead
Next to the trail 07817 502187

STOCKPORT - PENISTONE

Bridleway option from Kirkburton
See pgs 54-55

option
Kirkburton
gs 54-55

At Dunford Bridge

❶ Route Notes ★ See & Do ❶ Sleep ⛺ Campsite ❶ Eat ❶ Cycle Shops ❶ (with cafe)

Penistone

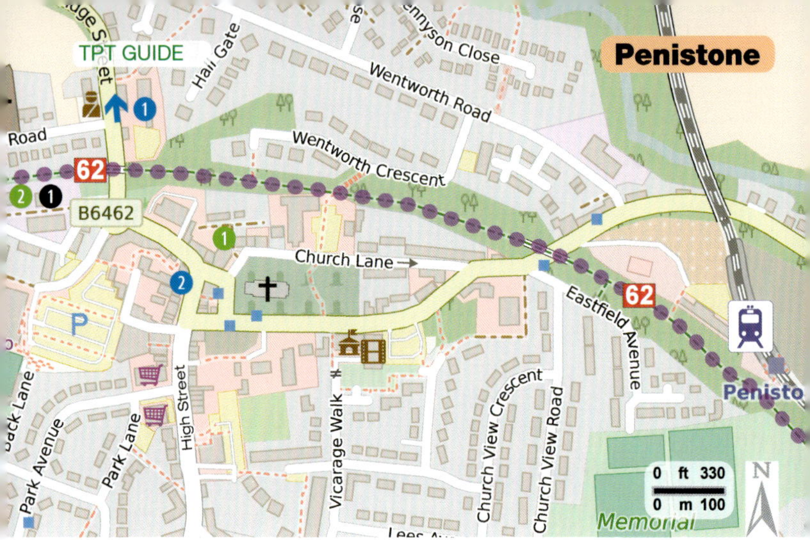

★ Penistone
Homely little Pennine town with a choice of cafes and pubs and with markets Thursday and Saturday. Picturesque St Johns Church.

① CUBLEY HALL INN
Mortimer Road, Penistone S36 9DF
01226 766086   cubleyhall.co.uk

② OLD CROWN INN
6 Market Street, Penistone S36 6BZ
01226 766609   theoldcrowninn.com

① ART HOUSE
Cycle friendly cafe and deli

② JULIE'S CAFE
Next to the trail

① CYCLE WORKS YORKSHIRE
Unit 1, Old Goods Yard, St Marys St, Penistone S36 6DT (accessible from the TPT too)
01484 794042
cycleworksyorkshire.co.uk   Servicing and repairs

Magnificent Pennine scenery around Penistone

STOCKPORT - PENISTONE

Penistone

 Route Notes See & Do Sleep Campsite Eat Cycle Shops  (with cafe)

STOCKPORT - PENISTONE

On Road Option to Kirkburton

1 The road route is generally very well-signed and easy to follow: pick it up by going L onto Hill Side Lane off the traffic-free trail, following NCN 627 signs.

Off Road Option to Kirkburton

2 At the next trail exit turn L down Leapings Lane (track) to a road. R is the footpath route to Thurlstone and L the bridleway route via footbridge and ford. The route is now generally well-signed. **Note: It involves some very steep and difficult climbs which mountain bikers may need to push up.**

3 At the main road over the footbridge jink R then L past St Saviours Church. Beware steps up climb!

4 Coming into Thurlstone split L off Royd Moor Road and L at road by Providence Church, leaving Thurlstone along Folly Lane.

5 Steeply dip and climb east of Royd Moor Reservoir. Keep bearing R to pick up tarmac and along New Row Lane meet the main road at Ingbirchworth.

6 Follow R hand side of several fields before picking up singletrack.

7 Take care leaving Upper Denby down Bank Lane; at a three way split follow the bridleway straight on (R and L are footpaths).

8 Leaving Denby Dale look out for the huge pie dish outside the school, just before you head off tarmac onto the track.

9 Leaving Shepley stay on the broad track, descending across a small bridge.

10 After turning R off the A629 turn R at the first L hand bend and follow the track through trees to descend to Kirkburton.

1 WOODMAN INN
Thunder Bridge Lane, Kirburton HD8 0PX
01484 605778   woodman-inn.com

2 THREE ACRES
Roydhouse, Shelley HD8 8LR
01484 602606   3acres.com

3 FOXGLOVE VINTAGE INN
36a Penistone Road, Kirburton HD8 0PQ
01484 602101   vintageinn.co.uk

4 MANOR MILL COTTAGE
21 Linfit Lane, Kirburton HD8 0TY
01484 604109   manormillcottage.co.uk

5 HEAPS HOUSE
11a Dearnside Road, Dendy Dale HD8 8TP
0774 0675831   heapshouse.co.uk

6 BAGDEN HALL
Wakefield Road, Scisset HD8 8SZ
01484 865330   classiclodges.co.uk/bagden-hall/

INGFIELD FARM CAMPING
Ingbirchworth S36 7GG
ingfieldfarmcamping.co.uk

MARSH FARM CAMPING SITE
114 Marsh Farm Lane Shepley HD8 8AS
01484 604448   campingandcaravanningclub.co.uk

1 THE GEORGE
Upper Denby

2 DENBY DALE
Good selection of cafes, pubs & takeaways

3 SHEPLEY
Cafes, pubs & takeaways

4 KIRKBURTON
Cafes, pubs & takeaways

1 TRY CYCLING
9A North Road, Kirkburton HD8 0NX
01484 607830   trycycling.co.uk

1 Route Notes   ★ See & Do   **1** Sleep   Campsite   **1** Eat   **1** Cycle Shops   (with cafe)

TPT GUIDE

Penistone - Doncaster

Route Info

26 miles / 42 km   Northern option   Off-road 23 miles / 37km
Height ascended 343m / 1125ft
28 miles / 45km Southern option Off-road 24 miles / 39km
Height ascended 429m / 1408ft

At Oxspring you have a choice of two routes. The more direct option leaves the Upper Don railway path at Oxspring, linking via track, road and path to another railway path, the Dove Valley Trail (latter can be muddy in places). Alternatively, you can stay on the railway path at Oxspring, heading south, following the Upper Don and Timberland Trails and the Elsecar Greenway on a variety of surfaces on lanes and bridleways. (harder to navigate than the Dove Valley Trail option). The landscape changes on this section as you pass from the edge of the Pennines proper around Penistone into rolling green countryside. The Dearne valley is a surprise to many - there are some very scenic sections culminating at the lovely Don Gorge between Conisbrough and the outskirts of Doncaster.

Track surface is a mixture of unsurfaced (possible muddy patches after rain) and some fine tarmac (mainly on the northern option, south of Barnsley).

Elsecar Industrial Heritage Centre

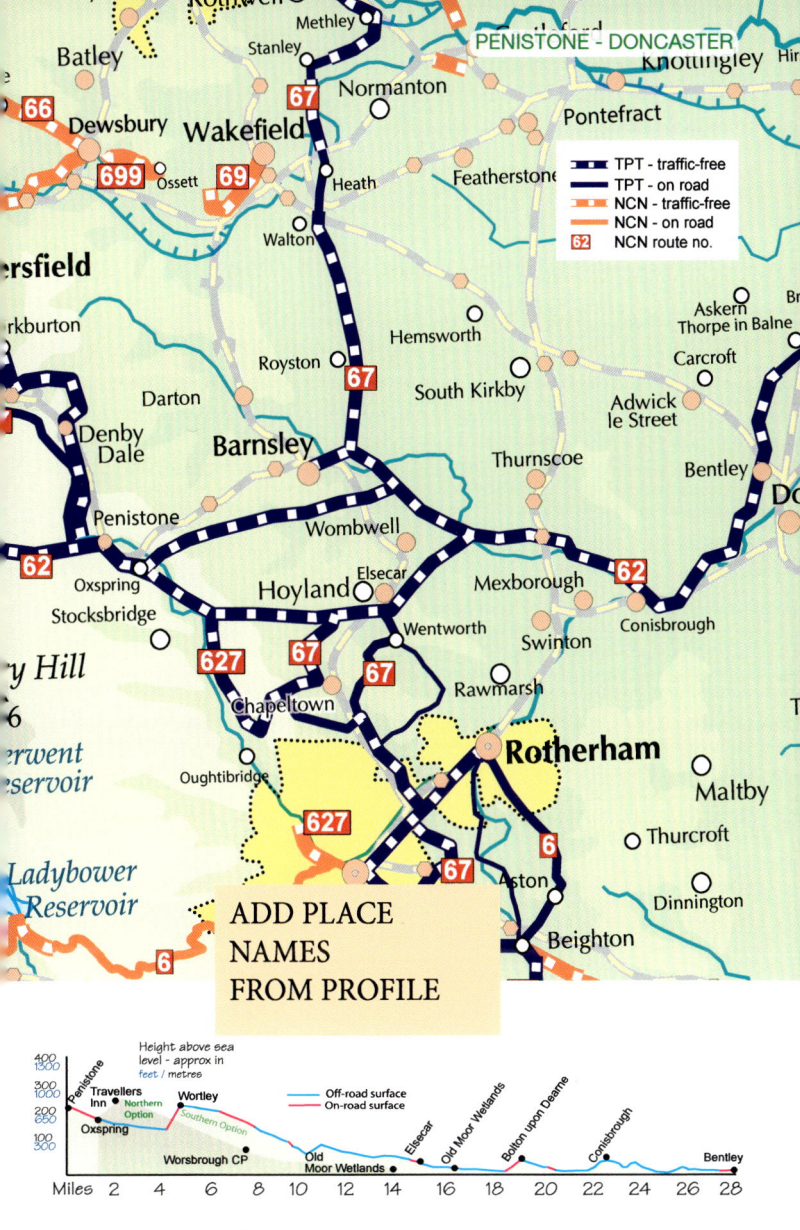

Worsbrough Mill

Don't Miss

- **Wentworth Castle Gardens** are just off the Dove Valley Trail and feature extensive parkland and gardens, subject to a recent huge restoration project. The house itself is not regularly open to visitors as it houses Northern College. Take a break at the Long Barn Cafe.

- **Worsbrough Mill Country Park** This 17th century mill still operates and its water-powered workings are a sight to behold. Set in 240 acres of parkland right next to the Dove Valley Trail. You can buy stone-ground flour made by the mill or sample the Millers tea-room offerings (takeaway food too).

- **Old Moor RSPB reserve** lies right on the TPT just after the Dove Valley and Elsecar Greenways meet and boasts plenty of beautiful wildlife and in particular birdlife, with kingfishers, avocets and marsh harriers amongst the star species. Cafe on site with free entry. Entry to the reserve free to RSPB members or chargeable otherwise.

PENISTONE - DONCASTER

- Although a former home of the Earls of Wharncliffe, 19th centrury **Wortley Hall** is actually now owned by a cooperative union and all proceeds go back to maintaining the hall and magnificent gardens.
Cycle down the grand entrance drive to take a look at the gardens with superb views over the Vale of Worsbrough or enjoy food and drink out on the terrace or in the bar. It's hard to believe that it was suffering from severe neglect as recently as the 1950s.

- **Elsecar Industrial Heritage Centre** is an imposing complex of buildings forming a huge courtyard and based around an 18th century coal and ironworks. Preserved and restored by Barnsley Council, today it houses myriad attractions including a children's play room, craft workshops and antiques centres, a unique Newcomen beam engine. Cafes.

- **Conisbrough Castle** has 12th century medieval remains today owned by English Heritage. A well-preserved keep is surrounded by crumbling walls and large expanses of grass ideal for picnicking. Entrance fee applies.

Elsecar Industrial Heritage Centre

TPT GUIDE

Route Notes
Route Split

1 Around 1.6km (1mile) after Penistone train station on the trail the northern trail option splits off L up a ramp, signed Oxspring (straight on is for the southern option along the Upper Don Trail).
The northern option itself has two route options, one on-road, one over lovely Willow Bridge then up a steep bridleway, both joining at the Travellers Inn.

Northern Option

2 At Blacker Green Lane bridge head R into woods onto singletrack.

Southern Option

3 Around 4.5km (3 miles) on the Upper Don Trail after the Oxspring route split, split L on the edge of Wharncliffe Woods, leaving NCN627 to follow signs for the Timberland Trail (actually NCN67). Pass the trail car park and emerging at the road head L, and soon start climbing.

PENISTONE - DONCASTER

★ *Wortley Top Forge*
Former iron forge with working water wheels, power hammers and even a miniature railway. Open Sundays and bank holiday Mondays from Easter to early November.

★ *Wortley* 🍴
Pretty, central square with post office/shop, church, tearooms and pub. Impressive Wortley Hall does B&B and has bar food for non-residents.

① WINDY BANK HALL
Hill Top Lane, Green Moor
Sheffield S35 7DQ
07944 605850 homesweetholidayhomes.com
Self catering (2-4 people). Min 2 nights.

② WORTLEY HALL
Wortley S35 7DB
0114 288 2100 wortleyhall.org.uk

① TRAVELLERS INN
Four Lane End Pub food

② SILKSTONE COMMON
Station Inn and Cottage Bakery

③ BRIDGE INN
Cote Lane, Thurgoland (follow signs off trail for Thurgoland and Wortley Top Forge, going L downhill at road).

④ WORTLEY
The Countess tearooms, a farm shop, classy meals at the Wortley Arms and food and drink at Wortley Hall.

Also cafes at Wentworth Castle, Wigfield Farm and Worsbrough Country Park. The Strafford Arms pub is on the link to Wentworth Castle. See overleaf for more detail,

① WORTLEY CYCLES
Repairs & hire at the post office 0114 288 2179
wortley-cycles.co.uk

On the trail near Oxspring

● Route Notes ★ See & Do ● Sleep ▲ Campsite ● Eat ● Cycle Shops 🍴 (with cafe)

Southern Option

1 New Road skirts Tankersley and ends at a T-junction. Head R and shortly L onto Black Lane, which soon becomes a track.

2 Track jinks L then R near ruins of hall at Old Hall Farm. Shortly afterwards L onto singletrack and across the A6135, to pass through car sales yard.

3 90° L into woods (don't head straight on for the railway bridge). Woodland track tricky to navigate. Emerge from woods to cross small valley with horse steps.

PENISTONE - DONCASTER

⭐ *Wentworth Castle Gardens* 🍴
Gardens, parkland and Victorian conservatory. Admission charges.

⭐ *Wigfield Farm* 🍴
Working farm with traditional and rare breeds plus small petting animals eg chinchillas and chipmunks.

⭐ *Worsbrough Mill & Country Park* 🍴
Working 17th century water powered corn mill in 240 acres of country park Working water-powered flour mill.

1 HOLIDAY INN
Barnsley Road Dodworth S75 3JT
01226 329100   hibarnsley.com

2 DELF COTTAGE
Houndhill Lane
Worsborough Bridge S70 6TX
01226 282430   delfcottage.co.uk
Self catering

3 TANKERSLEY MANOR HOTEL
Church Lane, Tankersley S75 3DQ
01226 744700   tankersleymanorhotel.com

4 PREMIER INN M1 Jct 36
Maple Road, Tankersley S75 3DL
0333 3218467   premierinn.com

🏕 GREENSPRINGS TOURING PARK
Rockley Abbey Farm, Rockey Lane
Worsborough S75 3DS
01226 288298

1 STRAFFORD ARMS
Pub food on link route to Wentworth Castle.

2 WORTLEY
The Countess tearooms, a farm shop, classy meals at the Wortley Arms and refreshments at Wortley Hall.

On the trail near Wombwell

⬤ Route Notes   ⭐ See & Do   ⬤ Sleep   🏕 Campsite   ⬤ Eat   ⬤ Cycle Shops   🍴 (with cafe)

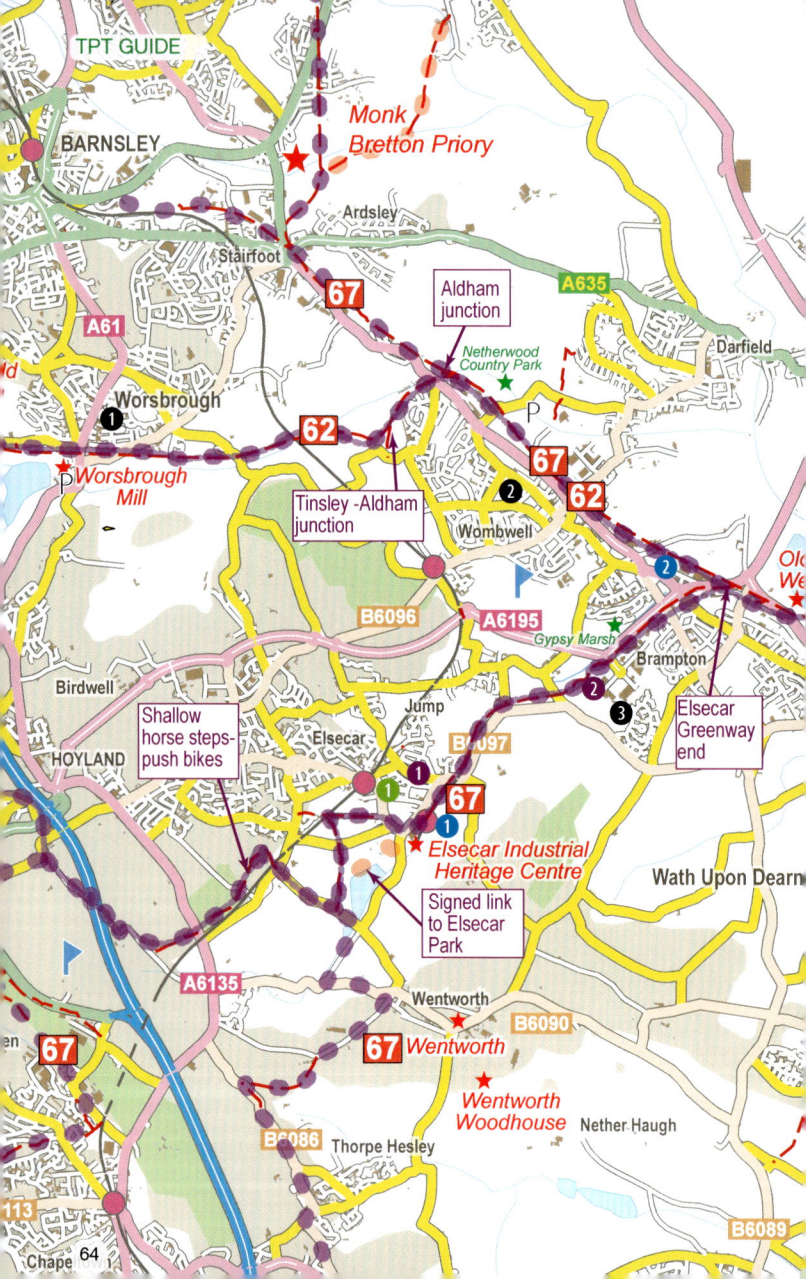

PENISTONE - DONCASTER

❶ R down the side of Elsecar Industrial Heritage Centre and immediate L after crossing the railway. Soon cross back over the rail line and head R to come alongside the lovely Elsecar Branch Canal on your left, now on the Elsecar Greenway.

❷ At a split head R away from the canal and come alongside the A6195.

★ *Elsecar Industrial Heritage Centre* 🍽
See *Don't Miss pg 59*.

★ *Monk Bretton Priory*
Just to the north of the northern route option, covered in the Barnsley - Leeds chapter. See pg99 for more detail.

❶ MARKET PUB
2, Wentworth Road, Elsecar, S74 8EP
01226 742240
hotelssources.com/market-hotel.html

❷ PREMIER INN BARNSLEY (DEARNE VALLEY)
Meadow Gate, Valley Park, Wombwell S73 0UN
0333 777 3679   premierinn.com

❶ ELSECAR
Budget cafe at the park, tearooms at the Industrial Heritage centre and the Milton Arms on or near the route

❶ BIKE TYKE
65 Park Road, Worsbrough Bridge S70 5AD
01226 233 432   biketykedirect.co.uk

❷ GEARED UP CYCLES
23 Barnsley Road, Wombwell S73 8HT
01226 756281   gearedupcycles.co.uk

❸ HALFORDS
Brampton, Cortonwood S73 0TB
01226 344010

The Elsecar Greenway

❶ Route Notes ★ See & Do ❶ Sleep ⛺ Campsite ❶ Eat ❶ Cycle Shops 🍽 (with cafe)

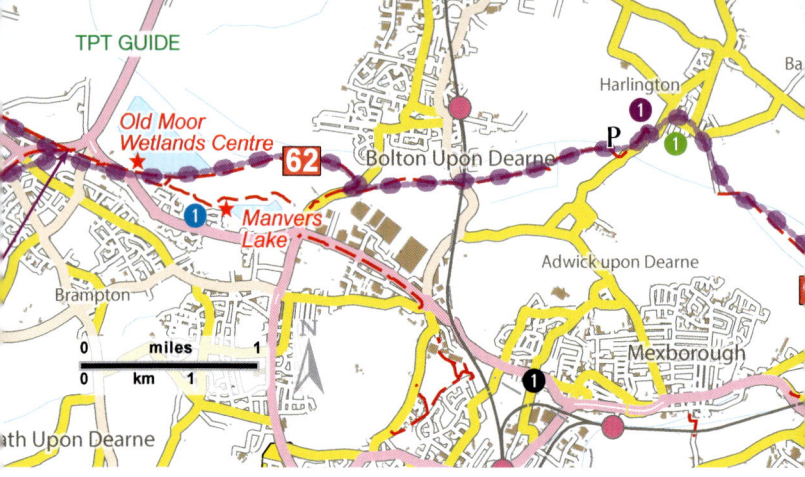

① About 350m after crossing the Dearne and passing through the car park turn R off main trail then L onto road. Next R in Harlington onto Doncaster Rd. After 450m turn R onto Mill Lane.

② Don't follow the path straight on across the spectacular Conisbrough viaduct; descend steeply to the L alongside the viaduct and bend L to come alongside the river Don, following a lovely section along the Don Gorge.

★ *Old Moor Wetlands*
RSPB Old Moor is the place to see a whole range of special birds For families there's a play area, nature trails and wildlife ponds.

★ *Manvers Lake*
Watersports centre in attractive setting.

★ *Conisbrough Castle*
Lovely restored castle ruins dating from the 11th century with picnic area and toilets.

★ *Conisbrough Viaduct and the Don Gorge*
Spectacular disused rail viaduct that you can cycle over (see route note opposite). Just before a beautiful section of TPT besides the Don.

① HOLIDAY INN ROTHERHAM NORTH
Express Park, Manvers Way
Rotherham S63 7EQ
01709 760666   ihg.com

② BEST WESTERN PASTURES HOTEL
Pastures Road Mexborough
Doncaster S64 0JJ
0333 003 4269   bestwestern.co.uk

③ HOLIDAY INN DONCASTER A1M
High Road, Warmsworth, Doncaster DN4 9UX
01302 799988   ihg.com

FERRYBOAT FARM FISHERIES CAMPSITE
Ferryboat Lane, Old Denaby DN12 4LB
01709 588088
www.campingandcaravanningclub.co.uk
Cafe in attractive setting

① HARLINGTON INN
Attractive pub en route.

② BOAT INN
Attractive pub en route.

① MEXBOROUGH CYCLE CENTRE
49 Wath Road, Mexborough S64 9QZ
01709 579249

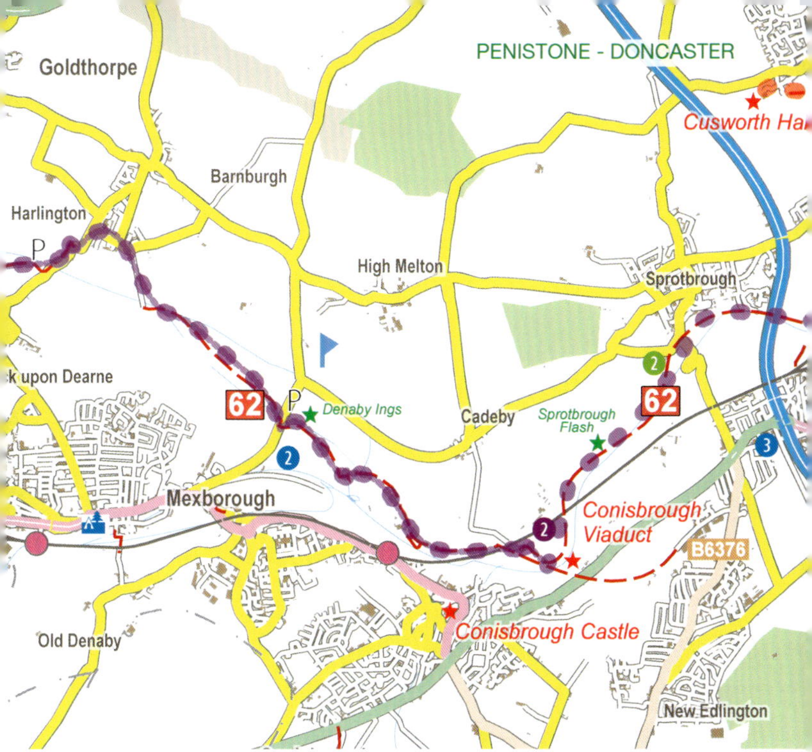

PENISTONE – DONCASTER

The TPT descends alongside Conisbrough viaduct

TPT GUIDE

① Just under the huge A1 road bridge head L away from the river.
② Ignore Doncaster and Warmsworth signs off L; the quicker and more attractive route heads straight on (signed Doncaster and Selby) and lets you visit lovely Cusworth Hall.
③ **Doncaster Centre Link** 500m after Cusworth Cycle Trail is signed to L (which links to Cusworth Hall) pass under A638 then in 400m Doncaster link turns R (easy to miss).
You are now on the Doncaster Greenway. Follow tarmac path to Centurion Way. Exit Centurion Way R onto cycle lanes to main roundabout. Head L, edging roundabout via toucan crossings to cross large footbridge and pick up cycle lanes towards Doncaster alongside North Bridge Road.
The main TPT heads straight up the trail and, 600m after the Doncaster Greenway junction, heads R onto Pipering Lane then L over level crossing into Bentley.

★ *Cusworth Hall* 🍽
Signed cycle trail leads from the TPT directly to the lake giving lovely views of the hall, an eighteenth century mansion. House and gardens recently totally restored. Old Brewhouse pub and brewery are located in the original brewhouse of the estate. Hall itself about 1km from route.

★ *Bentley Park*
Delightful little park with restored Art Deco buildings, formal flower beds and fountain in lily pond. Very near route in Bentley centre.

PENISTONE - DONCASTER

① MERCURE DONCASTER CENTRE
DANUM HOTEL
High Street, Doncaster DN1 1DN
01302 342261 mercuredanum.co.uk OK

② RED LION HOTEL
37 – 38 Market Place
Doncaster DN1 1NH
01302 732123 jdwetherspoon.com OK

③ PREMIER INN DONCASTER CENTRAL
High Fishergate, Doncaster DN1 1QZ
0333 777 4645 premierinn.com OK

④ THE REGENT
Regent Square, Doncaster DN1 2DS
01302 364180 theregenthotel.co.uk

⑤ EARL OF DONCASTER
Bennetthorpe, Doncaster DN2 6AD
01302 361371 theearl.co.uk

① BENTLEY
Small row of shops including a cafe en route

① FORWARD CYCLE STORES
87a High Street
Bentley DN5 0AP
01302 874164

② HALLAMS CYCLES
17 High Street, Bentley DN5 0AA 01302 874762

③ DON VALLEY CYCLES
203 Carr House Road DN4 5HG
01302 769531 donvalleycycles.com

④ PEDAL POWER
153 St Sepulchre Gate DN1 3AW
07555 298875 pedalpowerdoncaster.co.uk

⑤ CYCLE SUPREME
7 Bennetthorpe DN2 6AA
01302 322888 cyclesupreme.com OK

The trail heads alongside the lovely Sheffield and South Yorks Navigation near the Boat Inn

① Route Notes   ★ See & Do   ① Sleep   ▲ Campsite   ① Eat   ① Cycle Shops   (with cafe)

TPT GUIDE

① Doncaster Centre Link

Heading into Doncaster on North Bridge Road cycle lanes cross the river, canal and railway. At Church Way, the town centre is straight ahead down pedestrianised Frenchgate and the station is R on cycle lanes that pass under the shopping centre via a road tunnel.

Doncaster
Large market town which still has an excellent market, some fine Georgian buildings whose crowning jewel is the Mansion House. Doncaster is also well-known for its racecourse (St Leger every September, last Classic of the year), the Dome leisure centre (swimming, ice skating and concerts) and the South Yorkshire Aircraft Museum, all a mile or so from the town centre.

★ Doncaster Markets
A collection of Victorian buildings comprised of the Open market, Wool Market, Fish and Goose Hill Markets that will soon feature and multi-million pound redevelopment of the magnificent Corn Exchange building. A great area for both cooked and fresh food.

★ Doncaster Minster
A Giles Gilbert Scott design with a clock by the same person who designed Big Ben. If you like Victorian gothic style architecture this is a superb example and entry is free.

★ Elmfield Park & Town Fields
High quality segregated cycle lanes lead down Hall Gate and onto South Parade where you will find pretty Elmfield Park and the huge expanse of Town Fields, both good spots for a picnic.

★ The Danum Gallery, Library & Museum
In the Civic & Cultural Quarter.

Ⓜ BICYCLE BUDDY
Covering Barnsley, Rotherham, Doncaster and Sheffield
07585 904 818 bicyclebuddy.co.uk

Cusworth Hall

PENISTONE - DONCASTER

Doncaster

1 Priory Place
01302 734309
visitdoncaster.com

Doncaster Minster © Doncaster Central Development Trust

● Route Notes ★ See & Do ● Sleep ▲ Campsite ● Eat ● Cycle Shops (with cafe)

71

TPT GUIDE

Barnsley - Chesterfield

Route Info

37 miles / 59.5 km
Off - road 33 miles / 53 km
Height Ascended 760m / 2493ft
Above figures are for shortest route option only

At Oxspring the TPT splits. The southern loop via Wortley, Tankersley and Elsecar rejoins the main line of the TPT just outside Wombwell, but before this you have several opportunities to head off onto the Chesterfield spur.
The first comes just before Wortley and the second at Tankersley. Both options lead through pretty, rolling green countryside and the large area of woodland north of Grenoside. From here the route picks its way through the suburbs of Chapeltown and Parsons Cross before slotting alongside the River Don at the massive, gleaming Meadowhall shopping complex (a disused railway line is being developed as a more direct alternative along this section). A smaller spur leads off the main route alongside the interesting Five Weirs Walk, towards Sheffield, ending just outside the centre. The main route continues south and is nearly all off-road, finally making an impressive entrance to Chesterfield along the lovely Chesterfield Canal.
There are also two link options from Rotherham. The easterly one follows mainly roads via Aston whilst the westerly one is more family friendly, following the Sheffield and South Yorkshire navigation for much of the way, to join the main trail at Meadowhall.
Route Surface:
NCN 627 out of Sheffield is all tarmac.
NCN 67 is generally well-surfaced and wide but unsealed, so potientially muddy after rain.

Railpath south of Rother Valley Country Park

TPT GUIDE

Don't Miss

- Attractive **Wentworth village** is right next to a magnificent 18th century **landscaped park and Wentworth Woodhouse mansion**, with follies, monuments and serpentine lakes accessible to the public.
- **Rother Valley Country Park** A wonderful blend of fun-filled water-based activities and nature reserves. Activities include water-borne inflatables, cable skiing and the chance to hire multi-person pedal vehicles to trip around the lake. Also mountain bike trails next to the lakes.
- Both **Rotherham and Chesterfield town centres** may not be high on many visitors' lists to the area but they both retain a good enough share of older buildings to create a pleasant backdrop to enjoy the end of an attractive traffic-free ride along either the Sheffield and Tinsley Canal or the Chesterfield Canal (see opposite). Rotherham boasts a fine minster, a 15th century Chapel on the Bridge (used in medieval times to give thanks for safe arrival in Rotherham), the Old Town Hall shopping arcade, a fine market and several pleasant pedestrian squares. Chesterfield is dominated by the famously twisted spire of its parish church and has an impressive open air market (and a good covered one) and the nearby Shambles has the lovely Royal Oak pub.
- **Magna**, the UK's first Science Adventure Centre, explores the elements earth, air, fire and water Inside you can have fun firing a giant water cannon, launching rockets, exploding rock faces, working real JCBs and experiencing the roar of the Big Melt show, a simulation of iron making in what was one of the world's biggest electric arc furnaces.

Rother Valley Country Park

BARNSLEY - CHESTERFIELD

The Chesterfield Canal Towpath

- **Sheffield** is synonymous with steel manufacture and several reminders of the once great industry remain. Foremost is the huge collection of metalware in the **Millennium Gallery**, the gallery itself being part of a very impressive £120 million regeneration programme. This in turn includes the lovely **Winter Garden**, the largest urban glasshouse in Europe and home to several hundred exotic plants. Nearby are the **Peace Gardens**, a mixture of fountains, memorials, lawns and gardens.

Other interesting spots include the **Anglican Cathedral**, the canal basin and **Kelham Island Museum** showcasing the city's industrial past. One less well-known is the unusual and interesting **Cholera Monument**, found in the small patch of countryside behind the train station, with great views over the city centre. The Monument Grounds are the burial ground for most of the victims of the cholera outbreak of 1832, in which over 400 people died and the Monument was erected in their memory two years later. The monument is grade II listed and the grounds part of the Norfolk Road Conservation Area.

- The section of the **Chesterfield Canal** used by the TPT is in fact only the isolated southernmost section, but undoubtedly one of the most beautiful (the remainder runs east from Kiveton Park near Rotherham). Both Nona's Coffee shop at the Hollingwood Hub and Tapton Lock visitor centre (shop, refreshments & canal boat trips) are focal points in efforts to carry on raising funds for the 'missing link' as well as very pleasant refreshment stops and places to update yourself on the restoration progress!

Cote Green to Grenoside Option

1 Follow NCN 627 into Wharncliffe woods at the split in the track (Cote Green car park to the L). Signing is generally good on the broad track through the woods.

2 Track split here - go R.

3 Near Oughtibridge you pick up NCN 67 signs.

4 Leaving Wheata Woods at Grenoside head straight down Middle Lane and turn L onto Stephen Lane, to meet the main road through the village and R.

BARNSLEY - CHESTERFIELD

Tankersley to Grenoside Option

5 Follow TPT East signs out of Tankersley. At Tankersley Manor Hotel the TPT is signed through the hotel grounds, and pick up a track to cross the A616 on a small bridge. Cyclists and walkers route shortly bears R into woods, horses carry straight on.

6 Head up Bridge Inn Road then pass the Barrel pub on your L, and pick up traffic-free path again off School Rd / Blackburn Drive.

1 PREMIER INN
Maple Road, Tankersley, Barnsley S75 3DL
0333 321 8467 premierinn.com

2 TANKERSLEY MANOR HOTEL
Church Ln, Tankersley, Barnsley S75 3DQ
01226 744700 tankersleymanorhotel.com

3 FERNBANK SUITE
530 Penistone Road, Grenoside S35 8QJ
booking.com etc

4 WHITLEY HALL HOTEL
Elliott Lane, Grenoside S35 8NR
0114 2454444 whitleyhall.com

1 THE BARREL
Chapeltown. Pub food.

2 GRENOSIDE
Boasts the Village Cafe, three pubs and a fish & chip shop.

Attractive Grenoside

TPT GUIDE

Wentworth to Meadowhall Option
(road and track route - there are walking and horseriding braids too)

❶ Exit Wentworth down Church Field Lane to pass church and school.

❷ Lane becomes a track and emerges at road by Hoodhill to R - you turn L.

❸ R up Barnsley Rd into Thorpe Hesley then R again at mini-roundabout. Horseriders route then joins from R at Red Lion.

❹ L onto tiny Butterthwaite Lane which descends through farm buildings. Shortly after it becomes an unsealed track L onto fine railpath which leads all the way to Meadowhall.

BARNSLEY - CHESTERFIELD

★ **Wentworth**
Attractive village with Victorian architecture next to the Wentworth estate. Wentworth Garden centre has coffee shop, restaurant and beautiful historic walled gardens. Pubs and restaurant in village too.

★ **Wentworth Woodhouse**
One of hte largest stately houses in Europe with a stunning 606 feet facade, the house is now open to the public. Also renowned for its collection of follies and monuments. Take afternoon tea in the Long Gallery.

★ **Elsecar Industrial Heritage Centre**
See Don't Miss pg 59.

❶ **ROCKINGHAM ARMS**
8 Main Street, Wentworth S62 7TL
01226 742075   greenekinginns.co.uk

❶ **WENTWORTH**
Options include hot sandwiches from the village shop, George & Dragon pub and The Bothy (at the garden centre) as well as the Rockingham Arms.

❷ **GREASBROUGH**
Pub food at the Milton Arms

❸ **THORPE HESLEY**
Pub food at the Masons Arms and Red Lion plus a Chinese takeaway.

Magnificent Wentworth Woodhouse

Grenoside to Meadowhall

① Turn L onto Cowper Avenue off Fox Hill Lane. Descend to cross Halifax Rd onto Deerlands Av. **Signing generally very poor through Parson Cross and towards Concord Park.**

② At the roundabout by the large Asda head S/O then L at next roundabout. Shortly pick up the traffic-free trail on the R.

③ Good tarmac path along Tongue Gutter before the climb towards Concord Park.

④ **Route Choice** NCN 67 runs to the east of the original TPT route which is via Concord Park. Link path easy to miss. Concord Park option much hillier and signage poor.

⑤ Western approach to Meadowhall descends steeply over golf course on an indistinct path before descent through Woolley Wood on a broader track.

⑥ Out of Woolley Woods R onto Ecclesfield Rd. Follow onto Barrow Rd. L in about a third of a mile to cross the railway and join NCN 67 by Meadowhall Travelodge.

Route Notes - Rotherham to Meadowhall (Rotherham map overleaf)

⑦ **Detour to Magna** At Holmes Lock L, signed Templeborough, through Blackburn Meadows Nature Reserve.

⑧ Head over tram tracks then immediate R onto shared use cycle track, picking up signs for Five Weirs Walk to Sheffield.

Route Notes - Rotherham to Rother Valley Country Park

⑨ From Bridge Chapel head out of the town centre by climbing up Corporation Street, following signs for Rother Valley Country Park and later picking up NCN 6 signage. See town map on pg82 for more detail.

⑩ Cross the ring road onto Pleasley Rd.

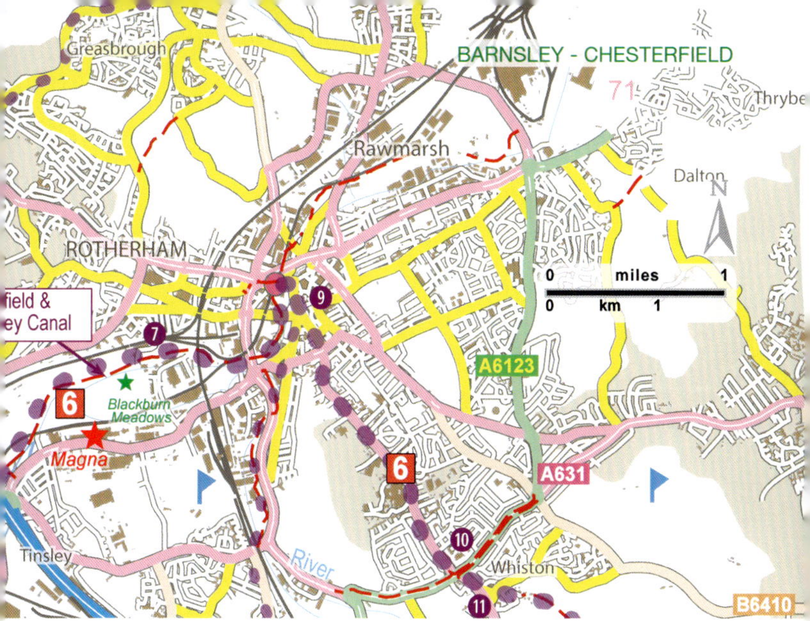

⑪ In Whiston L at The Green to climb on Doles Lane (soon unsurfaced).

★ Concord Park
Ancient cruck barn and sweeping parkland. TPT crosses Concord Park and then descends over golf club.

★ Meadowhall 🍴
Extremely large shopping complex with plenty of eateries and good train and tram links.

★ Magna Science Centre 🍴
See Don't Miss page 74

① TRAVELODGE MEADOWHALL
299 Barrow Rd, Sheffield S9 1JQ
0871 984 6435   travelodge.co.uk

② PREMIER INN MEADOWHALL Sheffield Road, Meadowhall S9 2YL
0333 321 8466   premierinn.com

Sheffield canal basin

● Route Notes ★ See & Do ● Sleep ⛺ Campsite ● Eat ● Cycle Shops 🍴 (with cafe)

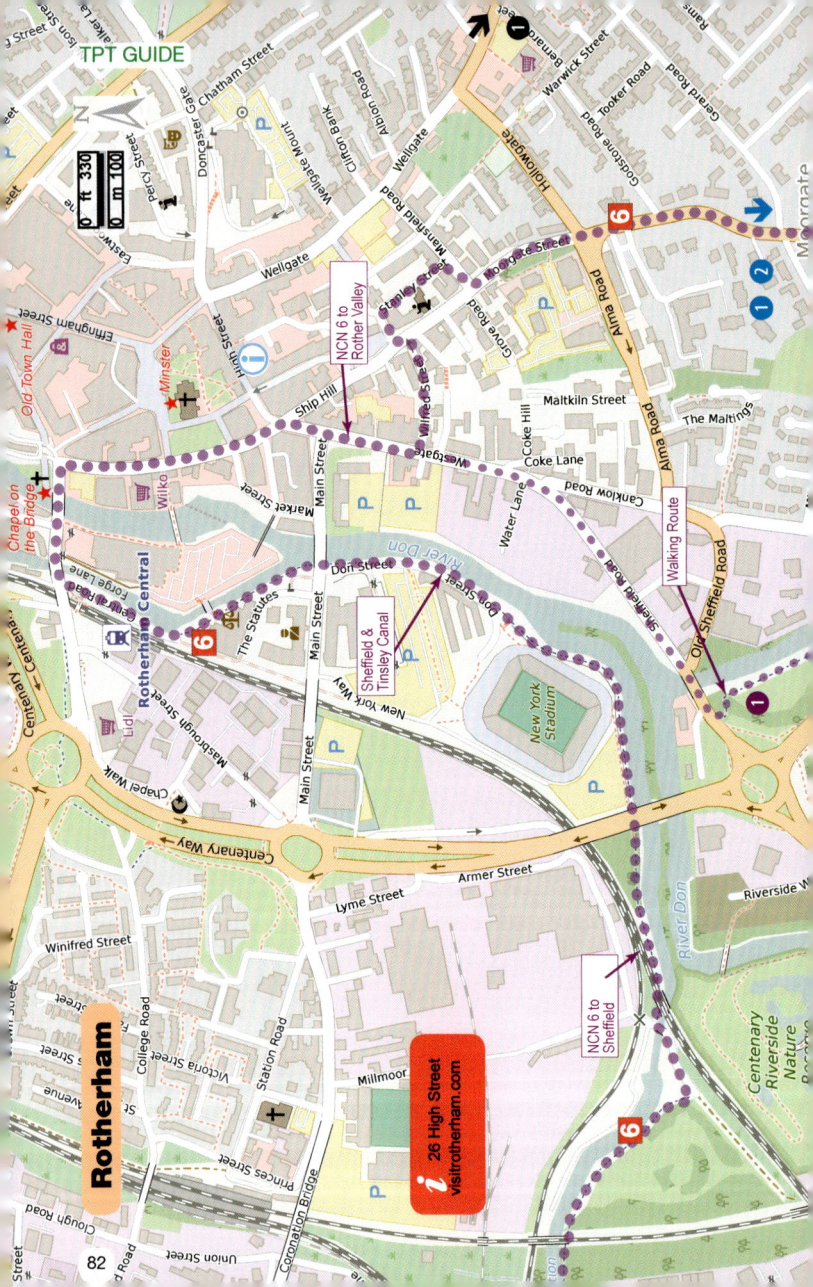

BARNSLEY - CHESTERFIELD

❶ The walking route out of Rotherham along river overgrown and poor condition. Walking route to Rother Valley generally poorly signed.

Rotherham
Another South Yorkshire town based on coal and steel industries but with a small attractive centre with plenty of architectural interest.
The Clifton Park Museum to the east of town has world-renowned collection of Rockingham porcelain and lots more for all ages.

★ Rotherham Minster
Lovely location above the town centre and surrounded by landscaped lawns and Minster Gardens.

★ Chapel on the Bridge
15th century building that fell out of use before becoming an almshouse, a jail then a newsagents before being converted back into a church.

★ Old Town Hall
Originally a Temperance Hall and Mechanics Institute this appealing building was converted to the town hall in the 1890s and now houses a small shopping arcade.

❶ CARLTON PARK HOTEL
102 – 104 Moorgate Road S60 2BG
01709 252232 thecarltonparkhotel.com

❷ BRENTWOOD HOTEL
114 Moorgate Road S60 2TY
01709 382772 greenekinginns.co.uk

❶ SONDEC CYCLES
222 Wellgate S60 2PD 01709 369607

Rotherham's Chapel on the Bridge

Route Notes - NCN67 to Rother Valley

1 Head off riverside path onto Carbrook Street. Split L onto NCN67 signed Darnall (Sheffield centre straight on on NCN6).

2 Good NCN67 signed cycle lane along Europa Link to enter woods. Through Bowden Housesteads Wood join NCN6 from Sheffield.

★ Ulley Country Park
Picturesque spot based around a small reservoir with sailing club.

★ Catcliffe Glass Kiln .
70ft brick cone from 1740. On walking route.

1 NOOSE & GIBBET INN
97 Broughton Lane, Attercliffe S9 2DE
0114 261 7182   nooseandgibbet.co.uk

2 HOTEL IBIS SHEFFIELD ARENA
298 Attercliffe Common S9 2AG
0114 243 4109   all.accor.com

3 PREMIER INN SHEFFIELD ARENA
Attercliffe Common Road S9 2FA
0333 321 8465   premierinn.com

4 TRAVELODGE SHEFFIELD RICHMOND
340 Prince of Wales Road S2 1FF
08719 846175   travelodge.co.uk

5 BEST WESTERN ASTON HALL HOTEL
Worksop Road, Aston S26 2EE
03330 034047   bestwestern.co.uk

SPRINGVALE FARM CAMPSITE
Morthen Lane, Wickersley, Rotherham S66 9JQ
01709 547346

1 WHISTON
Golden Ball and Chequers (pub food)

2 RICARDOS CAFE, Aston

3 BEIGHTON Fox Inn, Dollys Pantry (huge range of meals and sandwiches) & fish & chips

4 WHITBYS Fish & Chip Restaurant / takeaway (sitting out area). Between walking and cycling route near Catcliffe.

Route Notes   ★ See & Do   **1** Sleep   Campsite   **1** Eat   **1** Cycle Shops   (with cafe)

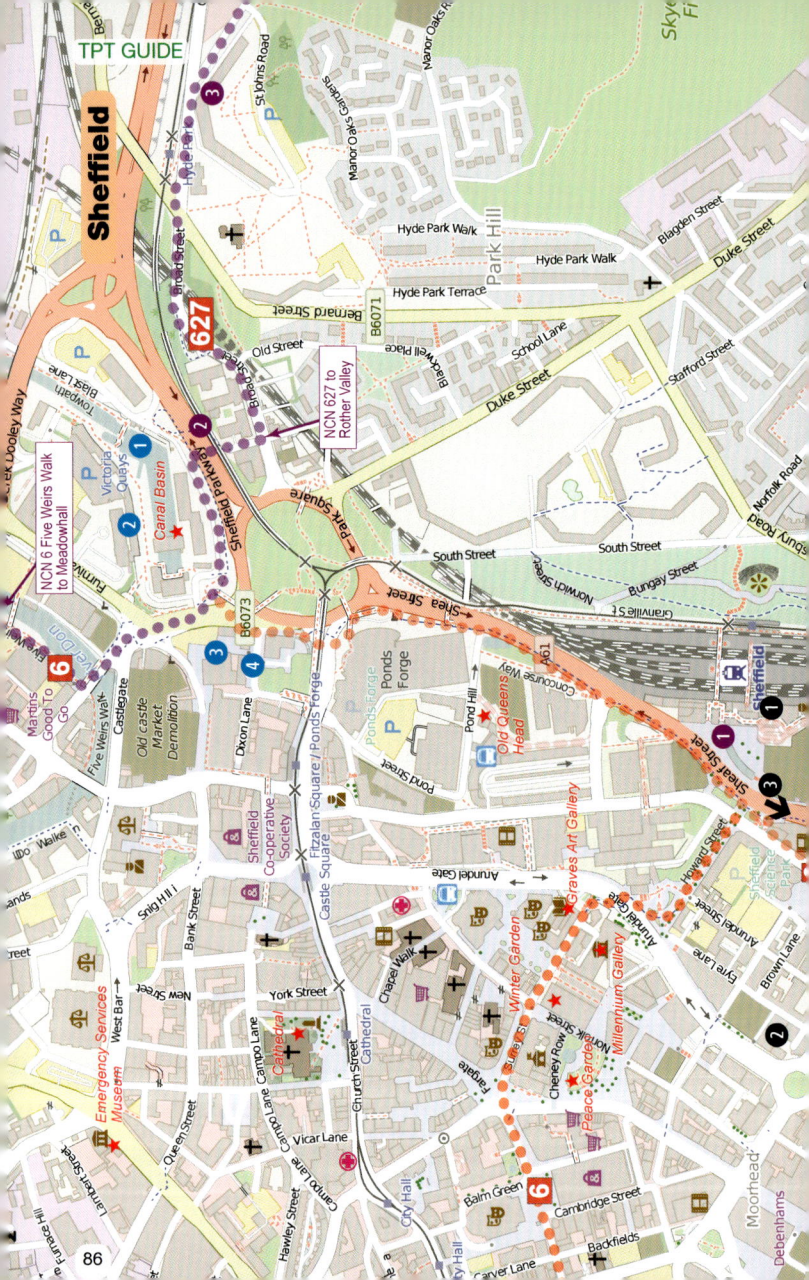

BARNSLEY - CHESTERFIELD

❶ If arriving by train follow signs for Five Weirs Walk on opposite side of main road outside station. Follow segregated cycle route to Park Square then signs to Rother Valley Country Park and NCN627, on far side of Park Square, out of Sheffield.

❷ Use subway to head onto Blast Lane.

❸ Pass Hyde Park tram stop and R down Maltravers Rd.

Sheffield
Known as Steel City and for knife manufacture and silver plate. WWII bombing destroyed much of the old town and the myriad steel mills have shrunk to a handful. Modern redevelopment includes a popular tram system.

★ *Peace Gardens*
See Don't Miss on page 75

★ *Old Queens Head*
Named after Mary Queen of Scots' decapitated head! Oldest domestic building in Sheffield.

★ *Sheffield Anglican Cathedral*
★ *Graves Art Gallery*
Above the city library. Outstanding modern art collection.

★ *Millennium Gallery*
Visual arts exhibitions & Sheffield's metalwork collection.

★ *Winter Garden*
Vast glass construction housing exotic plants next to a remodelled central square. The arched timber frame of the Winter Garden is covered by a 'skin' of glass which slides across the surface when the building expands or contracts due to temperature change

★ *National Emergency Services Museum*
A huge range of exhibitions, covering everything from the work of the Yorkshire air ambulance to an original Victorian prison cell.

★ *Canal Basin*
Picturesque spot with charter boats and house boats (including some you sleep on - see opposite).

❶ HOUSEBOAT HOTELS
Victoria Quays, Wharf Street S2 5SY
07776 144693   houseboathotelsheffield.co.uk

❷ BEST WESTERN PLUS QUAYS HOTEL
Victoria Quays, Furnival Road S4 7YA
0114 2525500   bestwestern.co.uk

❸ TRAVELODGE SHEFFIELD CENTRAL
1 Broad Street West S1 1AA
08719 846305   travelodge.co.uk

❹ HOTEL IBIS SHEFFIELD CITY
Shude Hill S1 2AR
0114 241 9600   all.accor.com

Sheffield centre hotels near the route in from the north east include the Crown Plaza Royal Victoria Victoria Station Rd 0114 2768822, Holiday Inn Express Blonk Street 0114 252 6500 and the Sheffield Metropolitan Blonk Street 0114 220 4000.

Around 2.5km from the route is an independent hostel :
RUSSELL SCOTT HOSTELS
Brandreth House, 28 Brandreth Road S6 3JU
0114 233 4691   rshostels.co.uk

❶ MOOR MARKET
Great selection of eateries and fresh food

❶ RUSSELLS BICYCLE SHED
Sheffield Railway Station, Sheaf Street S1 2BP
07787 641441   russellsbicycleshed.co.uk

❷ DECATHLON
199 Eyre Street S1 3HU 0203 1612920
decathlon.co.uk

❸ EVANS CYCLES
Unit 2 164 – 170 Queens Road S2 4DH
0343 909 2118   evanscycles.com

Ⓜ BICYCLE BUDDY
Covering Barnsley, Rotherham, Doncaster and Sheffield
07585 904 818   bicyclebuddy.co.uk

❶ Route Notes   ★ See & Do   ❶ Sleep   Campsite   ❶ Eat   ❶ Cycle Shops   (with cafe)

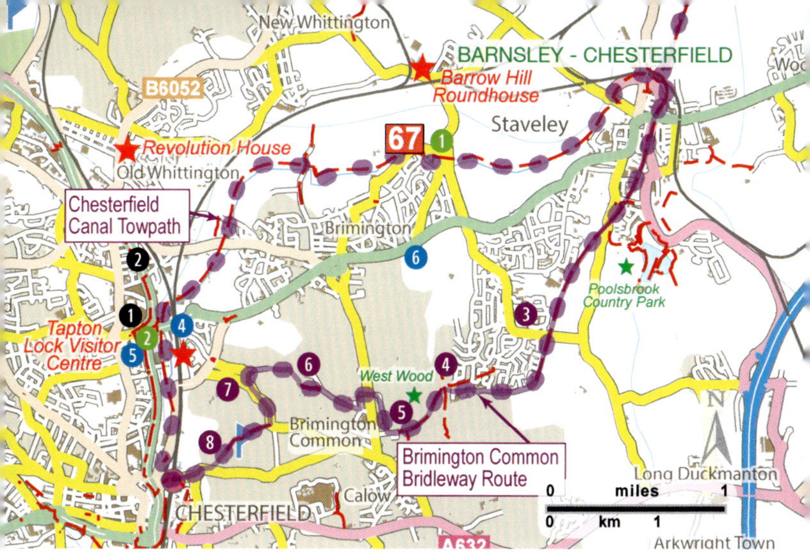

① Link to Rother Valley Country Park facilities

② Railpath splits here, just after crossing over a disused railway: **1** Easily navigable canal towpath route R or **2** bridleway route L, signed Poolsbrook Country Park. Canal option very shortly joins canal towpath, whilst the bridleway option continues on railpath past Poolsbrook Country Park. Note: Bridleway option includes lots more climbing and some rougher surfaces but has a great variety of scenery. Signing less consistent (some for Brimington Common, some TPT and some NCN67).

Bridleway Option

③ 2.7km (1.7miles) after the trail split near Staveley, exit L onto Bamford Road at Inkersall Green, signed Brimington Common & Chesterfield.

④ Leave Bamford Rd diagonally opposite Bluebell Close. Climb stony track to woods and head straight across into them. Main trail bends L and descends to bridge over little stream.

⑤ Skirt edge of woods and follow ahead out of woods. Shortly R onto Brooke Drive. At end of Brooke Drive jink R and L onto Recreation Rd. L onto Grove Way then R and follow ahead onto track.

⑥ L off track onto singletrack. Exit singletrack R onto broad track

⑦ Don't follow Paxton Rd but turn L to stay on Pettyclose Lane and after 500m R onto bridleway across golf course.

⑧ Leave golf course track onto access rd following to main rd and R to descend under railway bridge. Climb to rail station.

① HOLLINGWOOD HUB. Picturesque coffee shop by canal lock.

② Costa Coffee, Greggs, Subway and a Tesco cafe near the A61 roundabout at the western end of Lockoford Lane

① HALFORDS
 Unit 4, Netto Retail Park Sheffield Road Chesterfield , S41 8JZ0   1246 559897
② JE JAMES Brimington Rd Nrth S41 9AP
01246 453453

 Route Notes   See & Do   Sleep   Campsite   Eat Cycle Shops   (with cafe)

★ *St Mary and All Saints Church*
Twisted spire, due to unseasoned timber, dominates the centre. Monuments to the Foljambe family inside.

★ *Market Square*
Grand open space with regular outdoor markets including a flea market.

★ *Museum and Art Gallery*
Free town museum. Closed until 2025.

★ *Queens Park*
Cafe, lake, miniature railway and historic cricket ground hosting county matches

1 IBIS CHESTERFIELD CENTRE
Lordsmill Street, Chesterfield S41 7RW
01246 385050   all.accor.com

2 SPIRE VIEW AT THE GALLEON STEAK HOUSE
48 St Mary's Gate, Chesterfield S41 7TH
01246 559065
thegalleonrestaurant.co.uk

3 THE SPREAD EAGLE
7 Beetwell Street, Chesterfield S40 1SH
01246 234971
thespreadeagle.co.uk

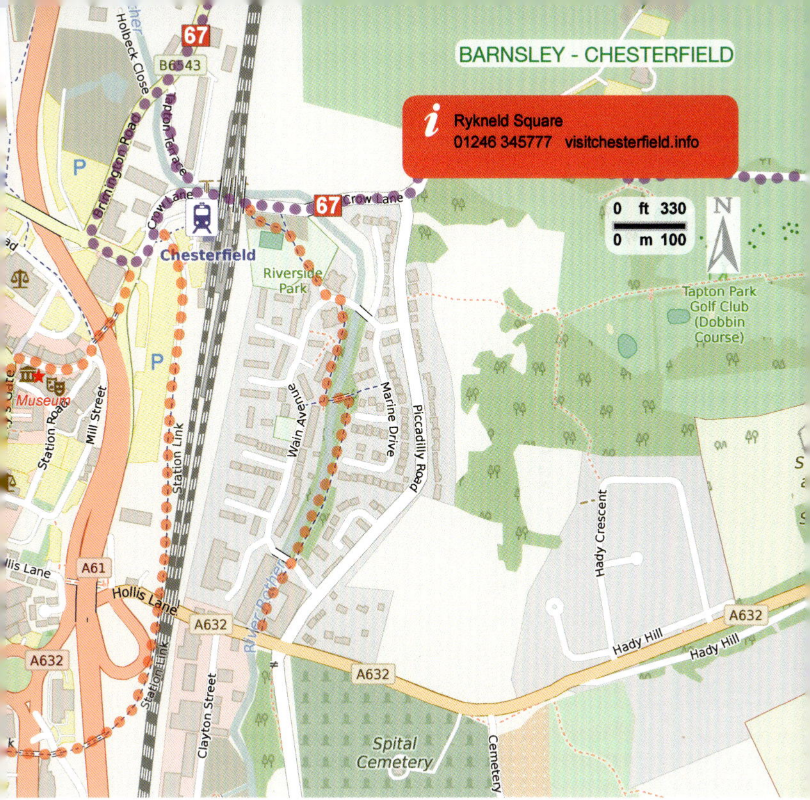

BARNSLEY - CHESTERFIELD

i Rykneld Square
01246 345777 visitchesterfield.info

0 ft 330
0 m 100

4 PREMIER INN
Elder Way, Chesterfield S40 1UN
0330 135 9039 premierinn.com

5 PORTLAND HOTEL
West Bars, Chesterfield S40 1AY

6 CORNER HOUSE APARTMENTS
18 Wharf Lane, Chesterfield S41 7NE
0745 6529339 booking.com etc

1 ROYAL OAK
Lovely historic pub on the Shambles.

M THE CYCLE SURGEON
07583 167575 thecyclesurgeon.co.uk
Mobile repair in Chesterfield and area

On the Chesterfield Canal

Route Notes See & Do Sleep Campsite Eat Cycle Shops (with cafe)

Barnsley - Leeds

Route Info

28 miles / 45km
Off - road 23 miles / 37km
Height Ascended 305m / 1001ft
Above figures are for shortest route option only

Although much of the line of this route might be associated with the collapse of the coal mining industry near Barnsley and Wakefield, it passes through some lovely green spaces.
The southern section uses the old Barnsley Canal. Highlights include the charming Heath village then the marina at Stanley Ferry on the Aire and Calder Navigation. Canal towpath is also used for your final approach into Leeds, arriving at the Royal Armouries Museum. There are braided links from here to the impressively redeveloped Leeds station.

The disused Barnsley Canal is now a rural retreat

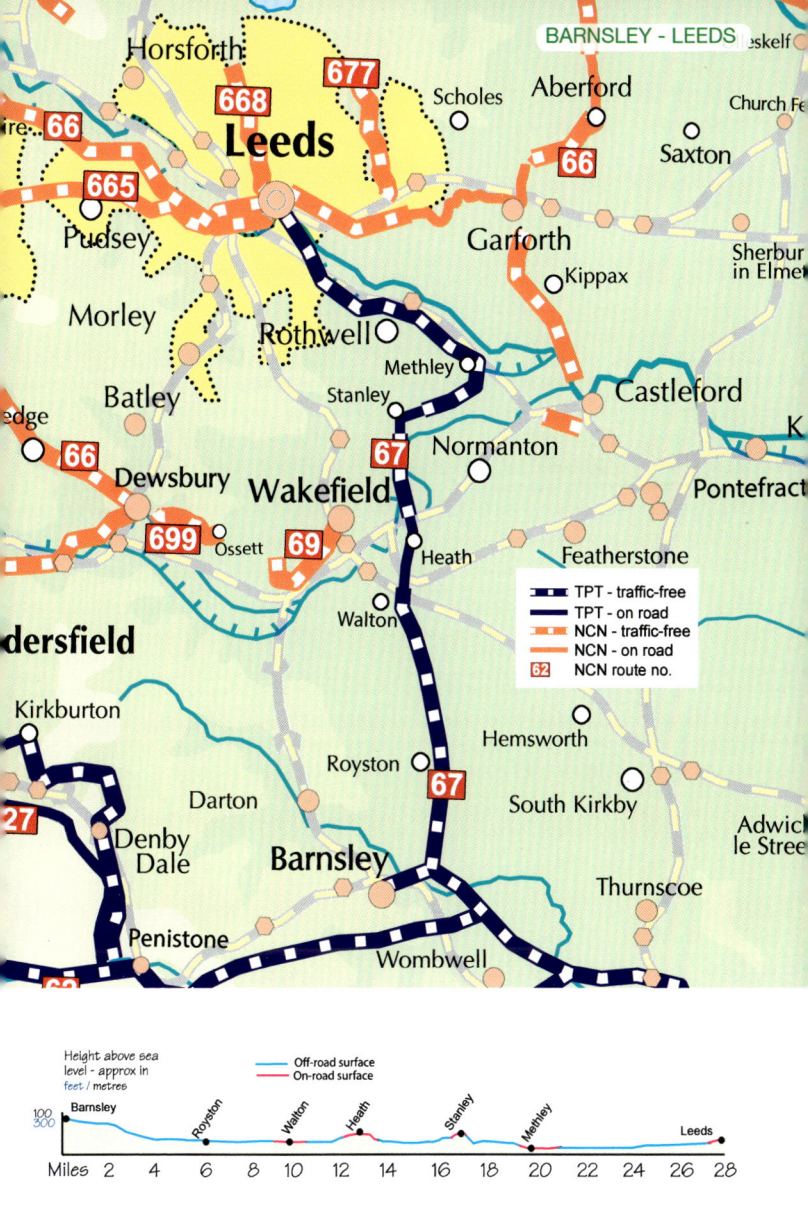

TPT GUIDE

Don't Miss

- **Haw Park Wood & Anglers Country Park** Haw Park surrounds a lovely section of the Barnsley Canal towpath which the TPT uses here and there are paths and bridleways off the main route linking to Anglers Country Park, a lovely lake surrounded by woodland and heath and with a small cafe.
- **Heath VIllage** Palatial size dwellings and smaller cottages set around lovely open green spaces, with attractive pub boot.
- Wakefield's **The Hepworth** houses an outstanding collection of modern art in a purpose built building by the river Calder. It's only 2.2km (1.4 miles) off the route near Heath Village and is accessed along the Wonders of Wakefield Cycle Route, a lovely ride through woodland leading to the River Calder towpath, emerging over a lovely little packhorse bridge on the opposite side of the road to the Hepworth. The gallery houses Wakefield's huge collection of modern art, including iconic works by Barbara Hepworth and Henry Moore.
The building itself was a notable new addition to Wakefield's skyline and there is a garden next to the main building. Cafe in entrance too.
Opposite the Hepworth is Wakefield's Chantry Chapel, a scheduled ancient monument and grade I listed building.

Walton village near Wakefield

BARNSLEY - LEEDS

The TPT passes the Royal Armouries at Leeds

- **Leeds Royal Armouries** is home to the national collection of arms and armour and is housed in an impressive setting between the River Aire and Leeds Dock.
The Hall of Steel is the architectural centrepiece of the museum, housing over 2,500 fighting objects which are ranged across its walls. As well as incredible objects like Henry VIII's armour and 17th century elephant armour there are also live shows of medieval combat, including jousting, archery and falconry.
Free admission and cafe.
- NCN 66 cycle route continues on south of the river Aire once in Leeds to the interesting **Granary Wharf** area, based around the dock at the end of the Leeds-Liverpool canal (itself a fine cycle ride). Here you'll find bars and restaurants and shops located in the railway viaduct arches. For a more full on shopping experience head to the town centre and take a look at the magnificent Kirkgate market or the sumptuous Victoria Quarter.
- **Walton to Anglers Country Park** has several attractions en route. From the New Inn at Walton the TPT heads off-road to join the Barnsley Canal, giving access to Haw Park Woods, Anglers Country Park and Waterton Park Hotel, set on its own island in a small lake.

TPT GUIDE

Barnsley

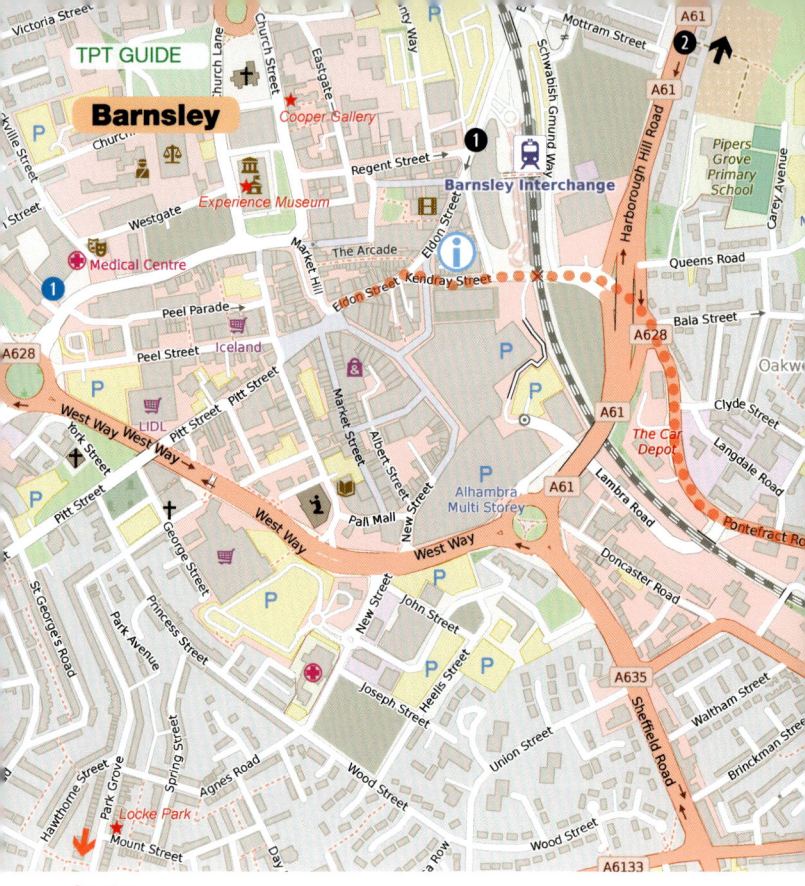

Barnsley
Once a coal mining town that has suffered much due to virtually total pit closure in the area. Local council originated the idea of the Trans Pennine Trail. Large food hall in market.

★ *Cooper Gallery*
Permanent and visiting exhibitions 01226 775678

★ *Metrodome Leisure Complex*
Theme based water rides ideal for kids

★ *Locke Park*
South-west of town centre. Statue of railway builder Joseph Locke and Italianate viewing tower in his wife's memory.

★ *Experience Barnsley Museum and Discovery Centre*
Free local museum crammed full of artefacts in a very elegant building.

① **PREMIER INN BARNSLEY CENTRAL**
Gateway Plaza, Sackville Street Barnsley S70 2RD
0333 321 9204   premierinn.com

BARNSLEY - LEEDS

❶ BARNSLEY ACTIVE TRAVEL HUB
The Transport Interchange, Eldon Street S70 1SD
07818 511133   barnsley.activetravelhub.co.uk

❷ HALFORDS
Dryden Road, Harborough Hill Road S71 1JE
01226 730640

Ⓜ BICYCLE BUDDY
Covering Barnsley, Rotherham, Doncaster and Sheffield
07585 904 818   bicyclebuddy.co.uk

1 Main route junction at Stairfoot. For Leeds option descend and cross road.

2 Cudworth link signed ahead. Keep L on main trail NCN 67.

★ *Monk Bretton Priory*

Substantial remains include parts of refectory, gatehouse and 12th century church. English Heritage property - free entry.

★ *Wentworth Castle*

See Don't Miss (pg58) and entry on pg 63.

1 TRAVELODGE
Stairfoot Roundabout, Doncaster Road
Barnsley S70 3PE
08719 846121 travelodge.co.uk

1 ROYSTON
Mini-mart and various takeaways.

2 MINI MARTS at this roundabout

1 RACE SCENE
High Street, Dodworth S75 3RQ
racescene.co.uk

1 EVANS CYCLES
The Peel Centre, Harborough Hill Rd S71 1JE
0343 9092750 evanscycles.com

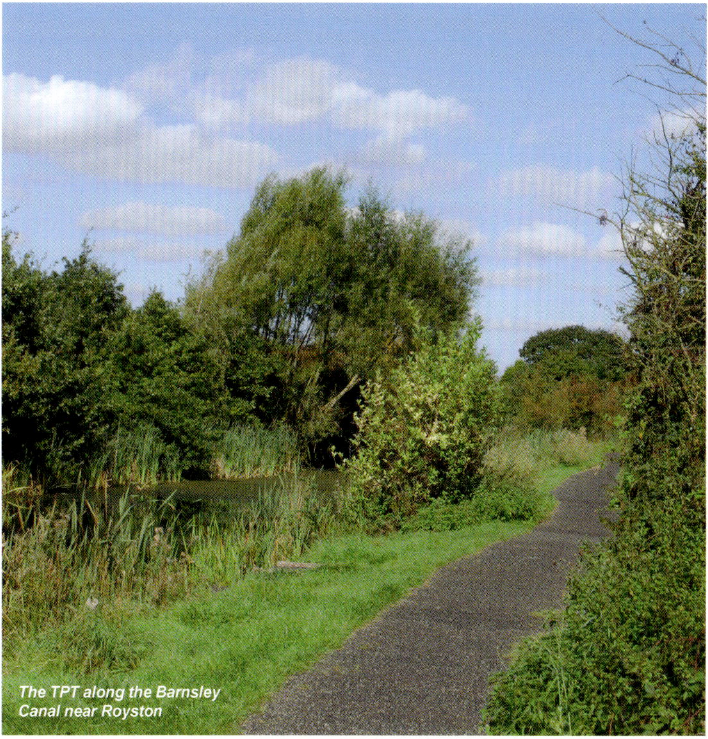

The TPT along the Barnsley Canal near Royston

1 Route Notes ★ See & Do 1 Sleep Campsite 1 Eat 1 Cycle Shops (with cafe)

BARNSLEY - LEEDS

① At Old Royston the trail briefly leaves the canal, going R across the railway then immediate L onto trail. Shortly after this a cycle link from Newmillerdam and Pugneys joins from the L.

★ *Barnsley Canal*
Towpath has been specially renovated for TPT use. It is now a very pretty section of the route, with reeds and wildlife having colonised much of the waterway and several narrow gorge-like sections.

★ *The Hepworth*
Follow the Wonders of Wakefield cycle trail to this major international gallery, about 1.5 miles from the main TPT. Cafe.

★ *Heath Village*
Large green surrounded by 18th century mansions with attractive nearby common land and cosy village pub.

① WATERTON PARK HOTEL
Walton Hall, Walton WF2 6PW
01924 257911 watertonparkhotel.co.uk

② THE REDBECK MOTEL
Doncaster Road, Crofton WF4 1RR
01924 862730 redbeckmotel.co.uk

③ HOLIDAY INN EXPRESS
Queen Street, Wakefield WF1 1JU
01924 372111 ihg.com

④ HOLMFIELD ARMS
Thornes Park, Denby Dale Road Wakefield WF2 8DY
01924 367901 greenekinginns.co.uk

⑤ YORK HOUSE HOTEL
10 Drury Lane Wakefield WF1 2TE
01924 372069 yorkhousehotel.net

① WOODLAND CAFE, Anglers' Country Park.

② ANGLERS' RETREAT pub

③ WALTON
Attractive New Inn, mini-mart and Chinese takeaway on trail and The Whisk Coffee & Cake shop, School Lane

④ THE REDBECK MOTEL
Cafe

⑤ HEATH VILLAGE
Kings Arms pub.

⑥ THE STANLEY FERRY
Pub grub

⑦ THE THATCHED HOUSE, Stanley

① CYCLE TECHNOLOGY
2 Calder Vale Road, Wakefield WF1 5PE
01924 311234 cycle-technology.co.uk

② HALFORDS
78 Ings Road Wakefield WF1 1TY
halfords.com

③ HOOD BIKES
Unity Hall, 83 Westgate Wakefield WF1 1EP
01924 665592 hoodbikes.co.uk

The TPT also uses part of the Wonders of Wakefield cycle route, as here near Walton

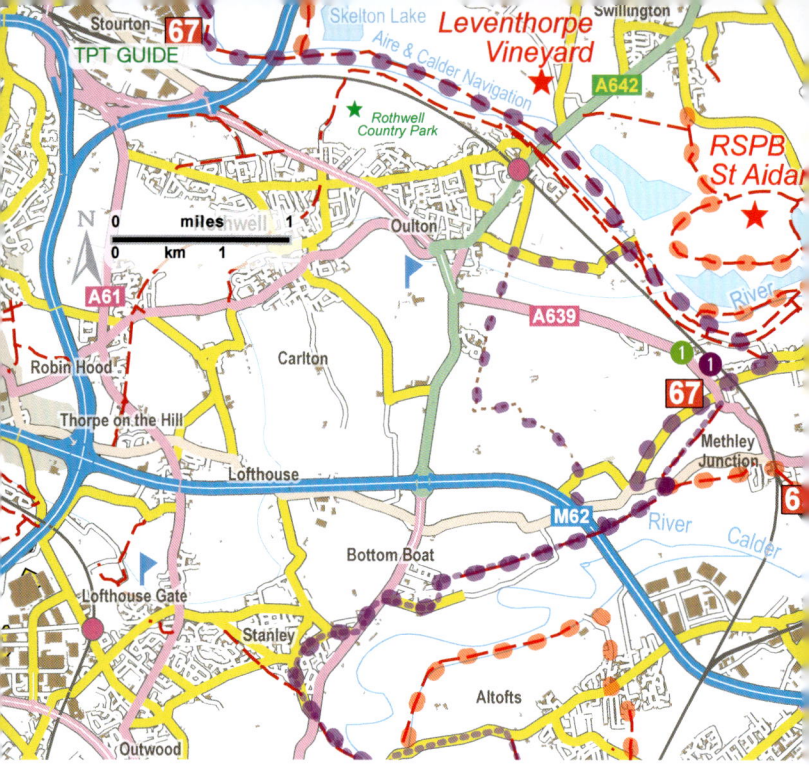

1 Turn L off Church Lane coming out of Methley, onto Mickletown Rd then straight over onto Station Lane. After joining the towpath and turning L here you follow it more or less all the way to Leeds. Be aware, however, that this section of the TPT has been prone to flood damage over the years and temporary works and diversions may well be underway.

2 Temple Newsam estate (see opposite) will be accessible from the TPT along a new traffic-free walking/cycling link. There is a new bridge over the Aire near Skelton Lake to make this possible.

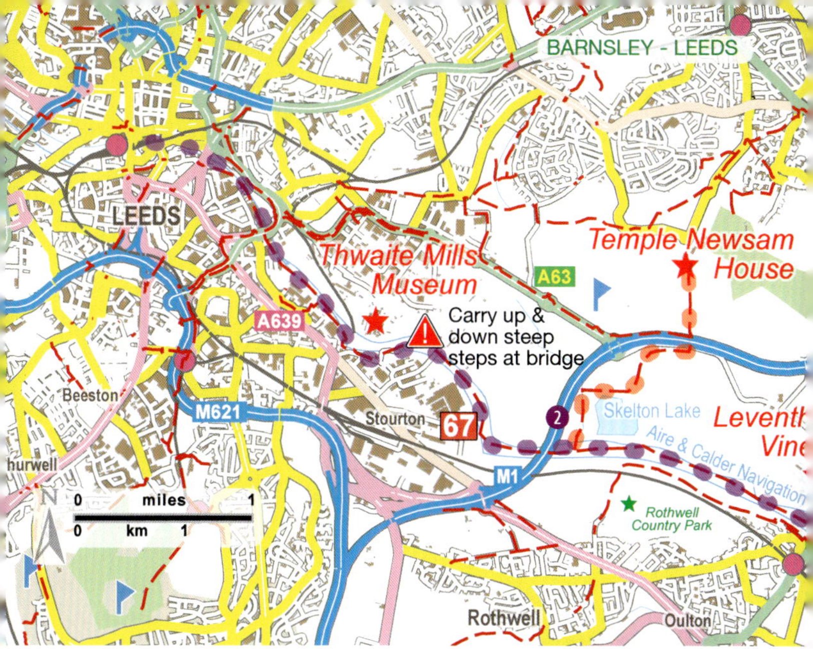

BARNSLEY - LEEDS

Carry up & down steep steps at bridge

⭐ St Aidan's Nature Park 🍴
An RSPB reserve with Little Owl cafe and toilets. Accessible via a network of footpaths and bridleways (on joining the towpath off Station Road just turn R, leaving the TPT, to access it).

⭐ Leventhorpe Vineyard
5 acre vineyard employs traditional methods and modern equipment producing white, red and sparkling wines

⭐ Thwaite Watermill
Original nineteenth century working watermill Previously a putty mill, now a museum with guided tours of the mill and engineers workshop

⭐ Temple Newsam 🍴
Large country estate, Tudor - Jacobean house, Home Farm, Rare Breeds Centre, walled garden surrounded by parkland, woodland and farmland.

1 RIVERS MEET CAFE Methley

In places the Aire & Calder towpath is a wide earth track.

● Route Notes ⭐ See & Do ● Sleep ⛺ Campsite ● Eat ● Cycle Shops 🍴 (with cafe)

TPT GUIDE

Leeds

1 THE QUEENS HOTEL
City Square, Leeds LS1 1PJ
0113 243 1323 thequeensleeds.co.uk

2 NOVOTEL LEEDS CENTRE
4 Whitehall Quay, Leeds LS1 4HR
0113 242 6446 all.accor.com

3 PREMIER INN WHITEHALL RD
1 Whitehall Riverside, Lower Wortley
Leeds LS1 4EQ
0333 234 6551 premierinn.com

Leeds combines a modern shopping centre with some grand Victorian architecture. City Varieties, Grand Theatre and West Yorks Playhouse mean a full helping of culture too.

★ *Royal Armouries Museum*
See Don't Miss pg95

★ *Centenary Bridge*
Elegant suspension bridge. Good view down renovated area of the Aire.

★ *Leeds Art Gallery*
Regional gallery with collection of British twentieth century painting and sculpture

★ *Market Hall*
Beautiful, complex structure of glass, iron and stone with a huge choice of food. Nearby Corn Exchange houses speciality shops.

★ *County & Cross Arcades*
Leeds is home to some of the finest Victorian arcades you will find anywhere, amongst the arcades at the heart of the exclusive Victoria Quarter shopping area.

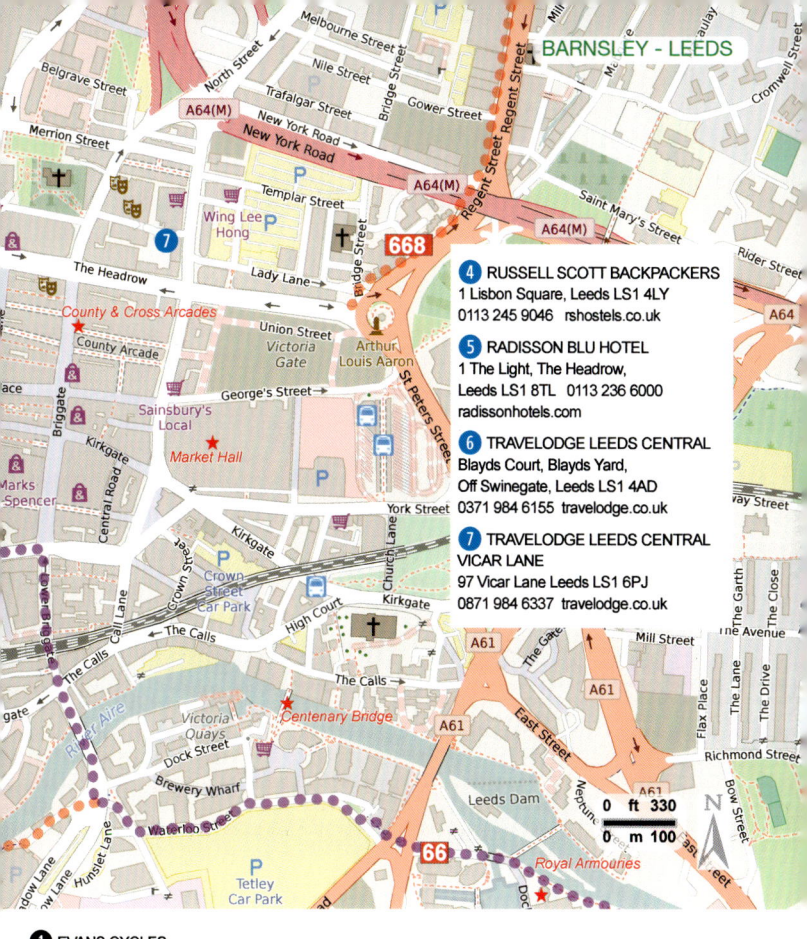

BARNSLEY - LEEDS

4 RUSSELL SCOTT BACKPACKERS
1 Lisbon Square, Leeds LS1 4LY
0113 245 9046   rshostels.co.uk

5 RADISSON BLU HOTEL
1 The Light, The Headrow,
Leeds LS1 8TL   0113 236 6000
radissonhotels.com

6 TRAVELODGE LEEDS CENTRAL
Blayds Court, Blayds Yard,
Off Swinegate, Leeds LS1 4AD
0371 984 6155   travelodge.co.uk

7 TRAVELODGE LEEDS CENTRAL VICAR LANE
97 Vicar Lane Leeds LS1 6PJ
0871 984 6337   travelodge.co.uk

1 EVANS CYCLES
14 Infirmary Street, Leeds LS1 2JP
0343 909 2357   evanscycles.com

2 DECATHLON
49 Boar Lane, Leeds LS1 5EL
0113 824 4130   decathlon.co.uk

Route Notes   ★ **See & Do**   **Sleep**   **Campsite**   **Eat**   **Cycle Shops**   (with cafe)

TPT GUIDE

Doncaster - Selby

Route Info

28 miles / 45 km   Off - road 10.5 miles / 17km   Height Ascended 25m / 82ft

Above figures are for shortest route option only

Pleasant red brick villages dot the flat agricultural land of South and North Yorkshire as you shadow the River Don, flowing north towards the Ouse. Agriculture's open expanse is broken by numerous huddles of trees, such as Owston Wood before a quiet road link leads onto the very peaceful New Junction Canal.
Minor roads and tracks lead to the Selby Canal into the market town of Selby, whose highlight is the outstanding medieval abbey.
This is a relatively quiet and sparsely settled section of the TPT, so it may well pay off to plan where you are staying and book in advance. Although there is a reasonable amount of accommodation in Selby there are fewer opportunities in the succession of small villages before this.

A taste of Holland on the New Junction Canal

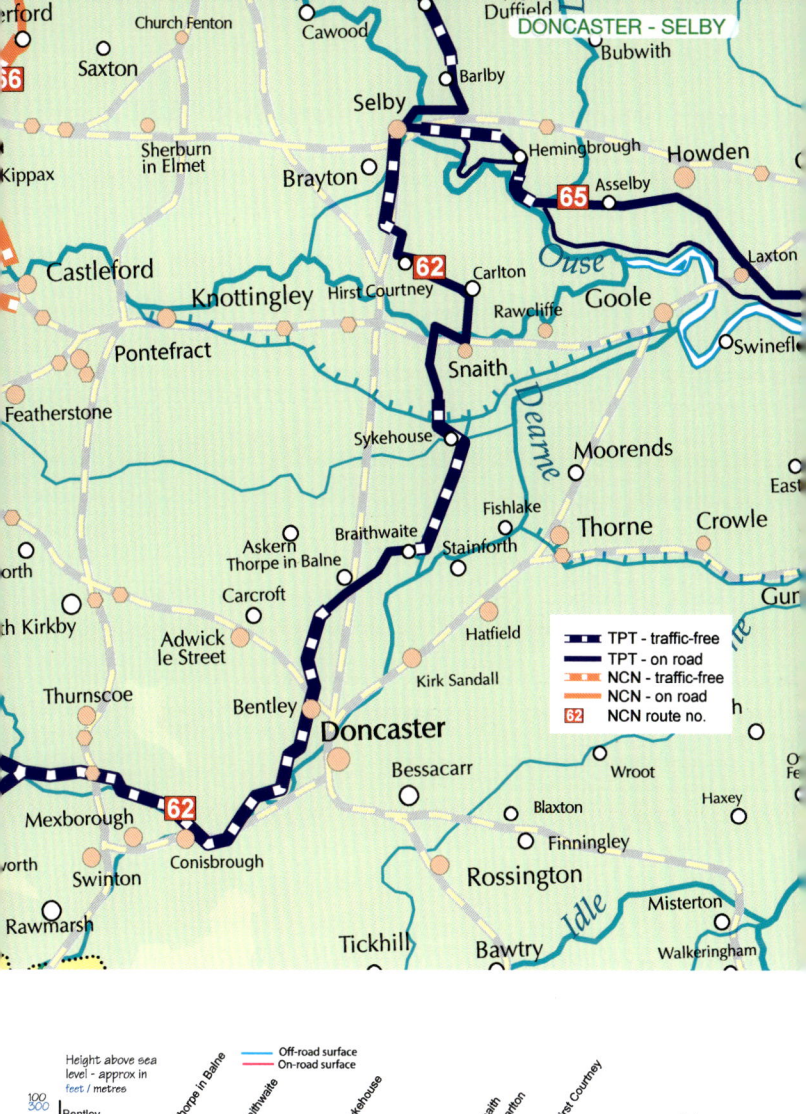

Selby Abbey

Don't Miss

• **Selby Abbey** dominates the centre of this small market town. Founded in Norman times, it is difficult to believe the beautiful structure you see today was the victim of subsidence, fire and vandalism in centuries past. The Abbey is open daily and also has a coffee shop, funds from which go to ongoing projects such as roof restoration. It has a carillion (an automatic device that plays out hymns from the abbey tower every three hours).

1 L off the main street in Bentley up Truman St then R to pick up a traffic-free path down the side of the park.

2 At the split before the road bridge ahead bear L and climb to the road. Turn L onto the road and shortly R, onto a minor road. This becomes a track by Tilts West farm.

3 At the 90 degree L keep on the main track and cross the railway at level crossing then into Owston Wood on the tarmac track.

1 THE OLIVE
1-3 Station Road, Barnby Dun DN3 1HA
01302 891403   olivebarandgrill.co.uk

1 BENTLEY, Cafe in small row of shops plus takeaway

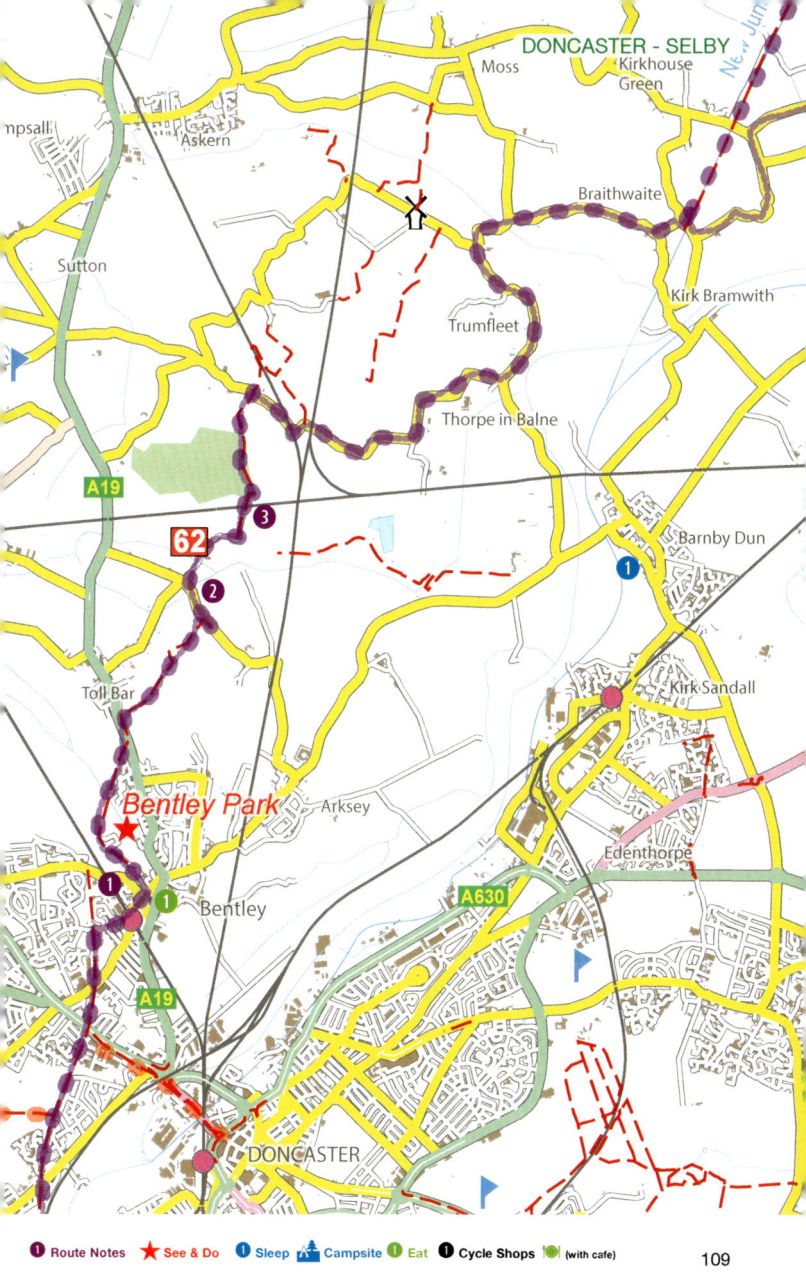

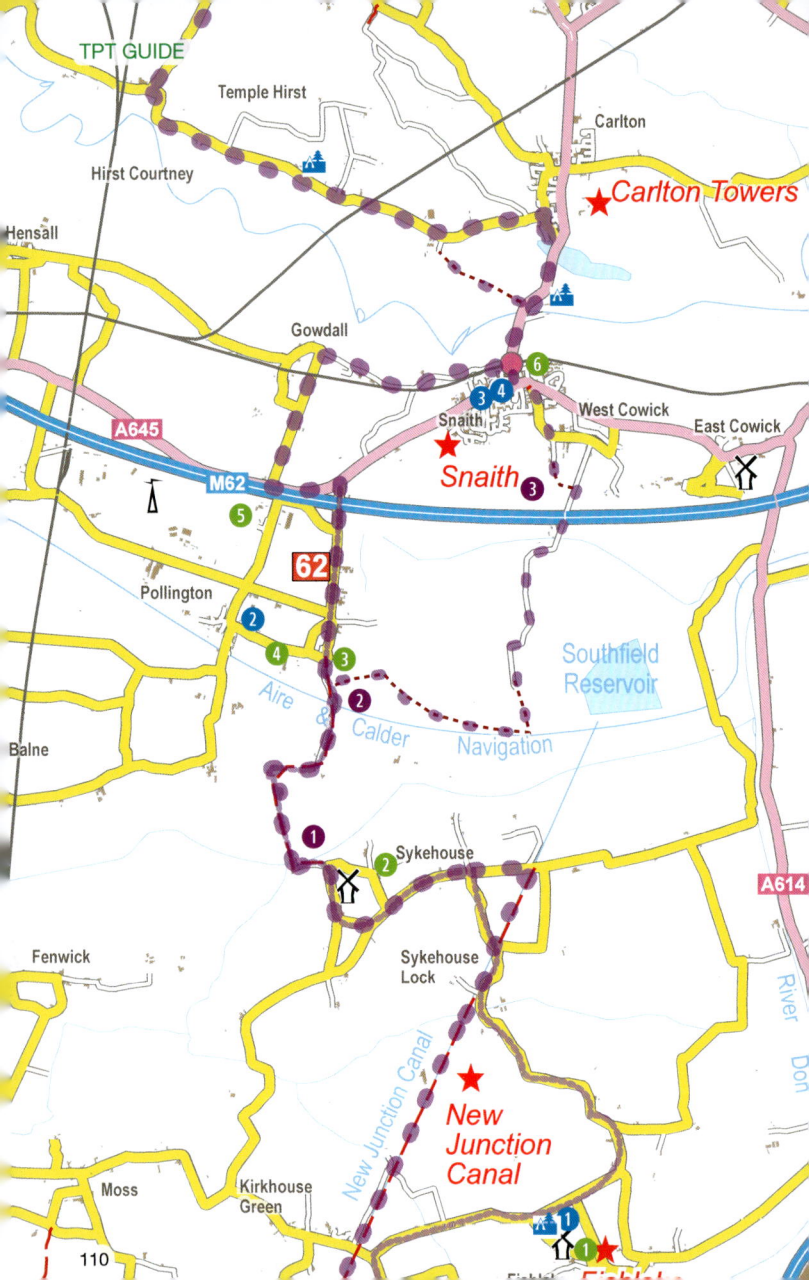

DONCASTER - SELBY

1 Head off the road and onto track across open fields to cross the Aire & Calder Navigation.

2 Walking Route Just over the canal turn R down track to follow canalside then field edge. Bear 90 degrees L, using fieldside paths which broaden to tracks.

3 Walking Route Cross the motorway and after 350m L onto path between fields. Bear R onto Spa Well Lane past the old brewery.

⭐ *New Junction Canal* This distinctively Dutch looking canal has only one lock and the TPT passes three distinctive lift bridges which make an interesting sight in operation. It was the last canal of the commercial age, dating from 1905, used mainly for carrying coal and some freight traffic continues on the canal. It links the Aire and Calder navigation to the Sheffield and South Yorkshire Navigation.

⭐ *Fishlake*
Village that was once an inland port. Info board by picnic area on Main Street. Picnic area was formerly a landing stage for fishermen on the once wide river. Ancient church doorway has extremely rare and fine Norman carving.

⭐ *Snaith*
Variety of shops and pubs Elegant church is the central village landmark.

⭐ *Carlton Towers*
Victorian Gothic mansion house. Once a conventional Jacobean House, it was turned into a mock medieval construction by two young eccentrics in the 1870s. Now a private building that you glimpse from the main road Occasionally open for weekend events

1 🏠 FISHLAKE MILL
Eastfield Road, Fishlake DN7 5LH
01302 841486 fishlakemill.co.uk.co.uk

2 PARKSIDE GUEST HOUSE
Main Street, Pollington DN14 8DW
01405 869759 parkside-guesthouse.com

3 THE BREWERS ARMS
10 Pontefract Road, Snaith DN14 9JS
01405 862404 oldmillinnss.co.uk/brewers-arms/

4 DOWNE ARMS
15 Market Place, Snaith DN14 9HE
01405 860544 the-downe-arms.co.uk

1 OLD BUTCHERS CAFE & BISTRO and HARE & HOUNDS pub, Fishlake

2 OLD GEORGE INN, Sykehouse

3 CRAFTY FOX TEA GARDEN Basic food & drinks, only open Sundays & bank holidays.

4 KINGS HEAD, Pollington

5 NANCY'S SITDOWN CAFE is north of Pollington signed '500yds' off the route (transport style cafe on an industrial estate).

6 SNAITH has several eating opportunities, including the popular Kitchen Cafe and various pubs.

🏕 SELBY CAMPING & CARAVAN SITE
Bridge Farm, Carlton DN14 9LN
07545 249964 selbycamping.co.uk

🏕
APPLE BLOSSOM CARAVAN & CAMPING PARK
8 West Bank, Carlton DN14 9PZ
07557 993074
appleblossomcaravanandcamping.com

Distinctive bridge along the New Junction Canal

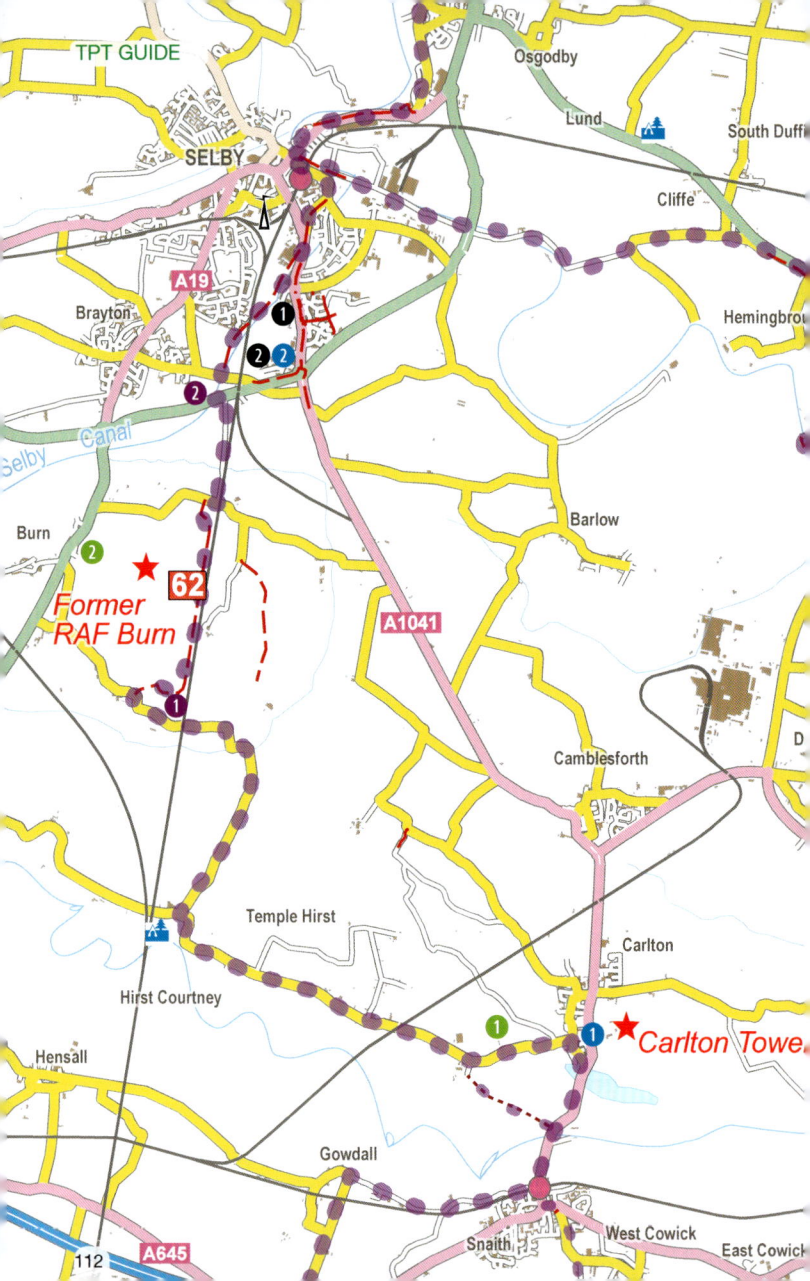

DONCASTER - SELBY

① R off road onto farm track, following signs to pick up track alongside airfield (beware glider cables when launching!). At the north end use path which meets the road where you turn R then L.

② Pick up the canal towpath at a small bridge (take care crossing bridge and obey lights).

★ *Former RAF Burn*
Little trace remains of the WWII bomber base from which bombing raids over Germany were launched in 1944.

① THE FORRESTERS ARMS
High Street, Carlton DN14 9LY
01405 860315

② THE WISHING WELL
Oakney Wood Drive, Selby YO8 8LZ
08712 003363
the-wishing-well.yorkshire-hotel.com

SLOOP INN
Main Road, Temple Hirst YO8 8QN
01757 270267

DOVE COTE LODGE CAMPING
Cliffe-cum-Lund YO8 6PE
07858 245586   dovecotelodgecamping.co.uk

① CARLTON NURSERIES
Carlton

② WHEATSHEAF INN
Burn

① HALFORDS
Unit C2 Bawtry Road Selby YO8 8LY

② HARD BIKE
Oakney Wood Road, Selby YO8 8LZ
07944 387668

Attractive Snaith

① Route Notes   ★ See & Do   ① Sleep   Campsite   ① Eat   ① Cycle Shops   (with cafe)

TPT GUIDE

🔴 Leave canal towpath to head R on Shipyard Road which becomes Ousegate. At the junction by Toll Bridge the TPT heads R and the town centre is to the L.

★ *Selby Abbey*
See Don't Miss pg108

🔵 HAZELDENE GUESTHOUSE
34 Brook Street, Selby YO8 4AR
01757 704809   hazeldene-selby.co.uk

🔵 GEORGE INN
Market Place, Selby YO8 4NS
01757 707355   greatukpubs.co.uk

You could also try The Unicorn on Bondgate (01757 841112) or Bay Horse Hotel on Micklegate (01757 428220).

🔴 COGS & COFFEE BIKE SHOP
30 Church Hill, Selby YO8 4PL
07434 770241

🔴 WILCO
Scott Road, Selby YO8 4BL
01757 210700

Canalside sculpture sign near Selby

Selby

DONCASTER - SELBY

Selby canal © Tim Green

① Route Notes ★ See & Do ① Sleep ⛺ Campsite ① Eat ① Cycle Shops 🍴 (with cafe)

TPT GUIDE

Selby-York

Route Info

15 miles / 24 km
Off - road 12.5 miles / 20 km
Height Ascended 104m / 341ft
Above figures are for shortest route option only

Flat agricultural land once again makes for easy going. There are a number of small, attractive red-brick villages near the route before the final passage of the TPT through Bishopthorpe and into the outskirts of York. Your approach to the historic core of York is a fine one, passing over the racecourse and alongside the River Ouse at Rowntree Park. After hugging the river through the centre you finish at the grand train station. Much of the section is on the excellently surfaced York - Selby Railpath, with path and road links at either end. Look out for the solar system trail along the way as you travel through a scale model of our solar system and the impressive Millennium Bridge in York.

On the railpath heading towards York

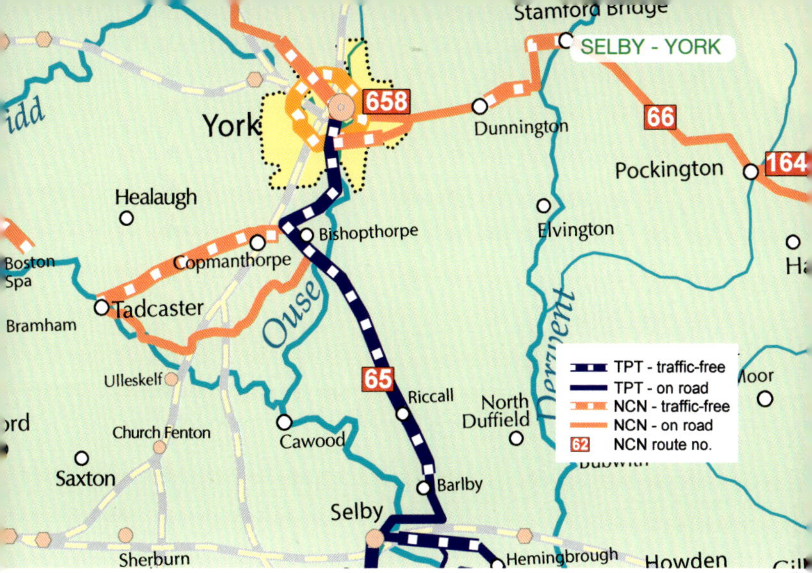

SELBY - YORK

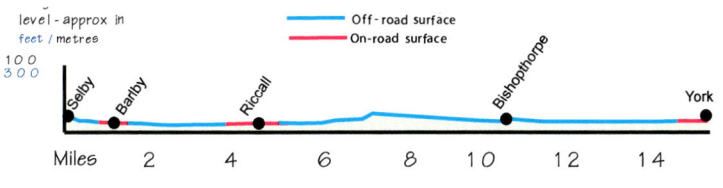

Millennium Bridge York

The River Ouse at York

Don't Miss

- **York** is one of the UK's premier tourist draws and it is not hard to see why. It's crammed full of wonderful historic buildings and much of the centre is pedestrianised, allowing visitors to roam at will and soak up the atmosphere. Pride of place goes to **York Minster**. It dominates views from many of the medieval streets leading up to it and inside the sheer scale of what is one of the largest buildings of its kind in Northern Europe becomes apparent.

In recent years some £23 million has been spent restoring the building, including putting right fire damage caused by a lightning strike in 1984 and more recently a complete restoration of the Great East Window. Nearby is the 15th century **St Williams College**, built for chantry priests who received payments for praying for the souls of dead benefactors. It also housed the printing press of Charles I during the Civil War.

Other highlights include **boat trips along the Ouse**, or walks and cycle rides along its banks, the **National Railway Museum** and many medieval streets and passageways, perhaps most famous being **The Shambles**. Kids will love the **Jorvik Viking Centre** or a walk around the **City Walls**. If you prefer green surroundings take a stroll around the **Yorkshire Museum Gardens**. Interesting eating opportunities include **Bettys tearooms**, always drawing the crowds. To avoid the queues try **York Library cafe**. **George Hudson Street** has become a centre for some fine restaurants.

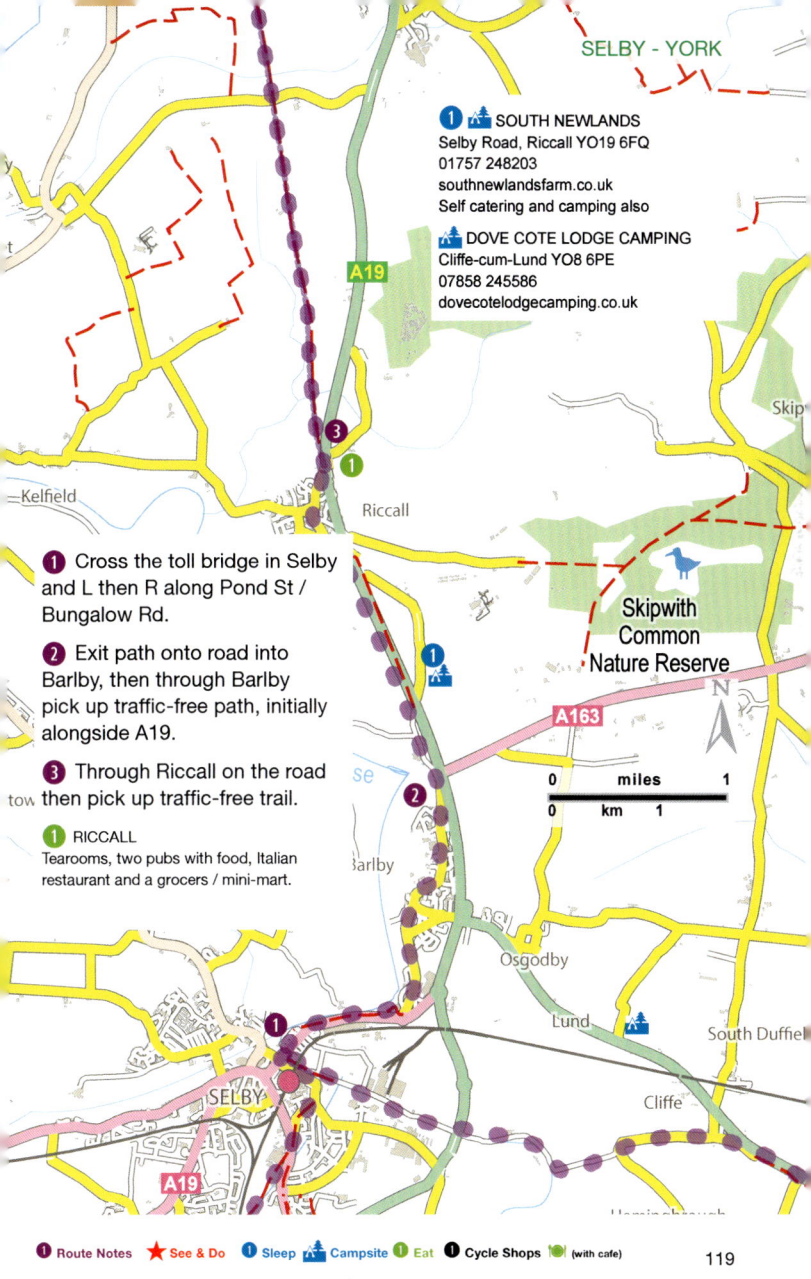

SELBY - YORK

1 SOUTH NEWLANDS
Selby Road, Riccall YO19 6FQ
01757 248203
southnewlandsfarm.co.uk
Self catering and camping also

DOVE COTE LODGE CAMPING
Cliffe-cum-Lund YO8 6PE
07858 245586
dovecotelodgecamping.co.uk

1 Cross the toll bridge in Selby and L then R along Pond St / Bungalow Rd.

2 Exit path onto road into Barlby, then through Barlby pick up traffic-free path, initially alongside A19.

3 Through Riccall on the road then pick up traffic-free trail.

1 RICCALL
Tearooms, two pubs with food, Italian restaurant and a grocers / mini-mart.

Skipwith Common Nature Reserve

Route Notes ★ **See & Do** **Sleep** **Campsite** **Eat** **Cycle Shops** (with cafe)

SELBY - YORK

① Railpath ends under A64. Bear R and follow to racecourse. Normally you may head across the racecourse but if its race day you can still pass by heading around the end of the track.

② Racecourse path ends at Bishopthorpe Rd. L and R onto narrow path to riverside. L to follow river into the heart of York.

★ *Naburn*
Lavish Ouse Navigation Trustees banqueting house just south of village cost £3,000 in 19th century!

★ *Bishopthorpe*
Grand Bishop's Palace Main buildings date from 15th century and chapel from 13th century.

★ *York Racecourse*
You might be lucky enough to head through here on the TPT when a race is on; race horses thundering past just a few feet from you are quite a sight. It's a large, rich racecourse with a lovely grandstand and the TPT lets you enjoy lovely views of it.

④ STABLESIDE
Tadcaster Road YO24 1QG
01904 709174 stablesideyork.co.uk

NABURN LOCK CARAVAN PARK
Naburn YO19 4RU
01904 728697 yorknaburnlock.com

MILLBRIDGE FARM CAMPING
Howden Lane, Naburn YO19 4RP
01904 656255

POPLAR FARM CARAVAN PARK
Acaster Malbis YO23 2UQ
01904 706548 poplarfarm-caravans.co.uk

See overleaf for following on map

⑤ ROOMZZZ
Terry Avenue YO23 FG
0203 504 5555 roomzzz.com

⑥ MIDDLETONS HOTEL
Skeldergate YO1 6DU
01904 611570 middletonsyork.co.uk

⑦ QUEENS HOTEL
Queens Staith, Skeldergate YO1 6DH
01904 611321 queenshotel-york.com

⑧ TRAVELODGE YORK CENTRAL
Micklegate YO1 6JG
0871 984 6443 travelodge.co.uk

⑨ PARK INN BY RADISSON
North Street YO1 6JF
01904 459988 radissonhotels.com

⑩ SAFESTAY YORK HOSTEL
88 – 90 Micklegate YO1 6JX
01904 627720 safestay.com

⑪ BAR CONVENT GUEST HOUSE
17, Blossom Street YO24 1AQ
01904 643 238 barconvent.co.uk

⑫ PREMIER INN YORK CITY
(Blossom St North)
20 Blossom St YO24 1AJ

0333 3219198 premierinn.com

⑬ PREMIER INN YORK CITY
(Blossom St South)
28-40 Blossom St YO24 1AJ
0333 3219197 premierinn.com

⑭ GRAND HOTEL & SPA
Station Rise YO1 6GD
01904 380038 thegrandyork.co.uk

⑮ FORT BOUTIQUE HOSTEL
1 Little Stonegate YO1 8AX
01904 202822 thefortyork.co.uk

⑯ ABBEY GUEST HOUSE
13 – 14 Earlsborough Terrace
Marygate YO30 7BQ
01904 627782 abbeyguesthouseyork.co.uk

⑰ YHA YORK
42 Water End, Clifton YO30 6LP
0345 371 9051 yha.org.uk

⑱ TRAVELODGE YORK CENTRAL
90 Piccadilly YO1 9NX
08719846187 travelodge.co.uk

TPT GUIDE

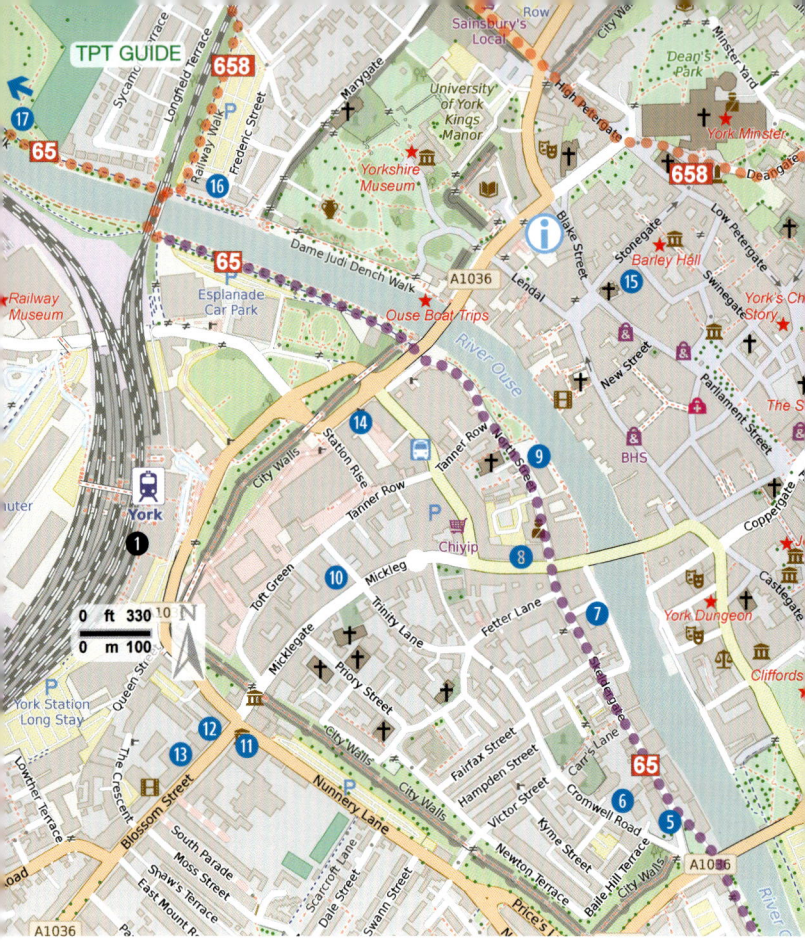

★ *York Minster*
The largest Gothic church in northern Europe, built over a 250 years. The Lady Chapel contains the Great East Window, the size of a tennis court, the world's largest area of medieval glass.

★ *Barley Hall*
Coffee Yard   Reconstructed townhouse of a medieval York citizen.

★ *Yorkshire Museum*
Perhaps the North's finest collections of archaeology and natural history

★ *National Railway Museum*
Includes classics such as Victorian and Edwardian royal carriages and the Mallard. Free entry

★ *The Shambles*
One of the best preserved medieval streets in Europe.

★ *Merchant Adventurers Hall*
Huge timber-framed building deriving its name from the powerful medieval trading organisation Open daily Admission charge

SELBY - YORK

York

21 Parliament St, YO1 8SG
01904 555670   visityork.org

Too many cycle shops in York to detail but amongst the best are
1. CYCLE HEAVEN York Rail station 01904 622701 with another branch just out of town (Hospital Fields Road).
2. YORK CYCLEWORKS 14 – 18 Lawrence Street YO10 3WP 01904 626664
3. ELECTRIC TRANSPORT SHOP 32 Walmgate YO1 9TJ 01904 623515 electricbikesales.co.uk
Also a bike recycling shops on Walmgate.

★ *Jorvik Viking Centre*
Recreation of a tenth century Coppergate alley

★ *Cliffords Tower*
Its name comes from Roger Clifford, hanged from the tower wrapped in chains in the 14th century Great views from the upper rim   Open daily

★ *Castle Museum*
England's most popular museum of everyday life, with period, reconstructed streets.

★ *River Ouse Boat Trips*
One of the best ways to experience York's wonderful riverscape.

★ *York Dungeon*
The history of the dungeon - gruesome entertainment that kids will love! Actors, sets and displays.

★ *York's Chocolate Story*
Chocolate was once as important to York as wool was to Bradford. Here is the full story plus plenty of tasting opportunities.

Route Notes   ★ See & Do   Sleep   Campsite   Eat   Cycle Shops   (with cafe)

TPT GUIDE

Selby - Elloughton & Brough

Route Info

28 miles / 45 km
Off - road 5.5 miles / 9 km
Height Ascended 116m / 381ft
Above figures are for shortest route option only

One of the quietest sections on the whole TPT runs parallel to the slow, wide Ouse through some tiny villages to the base of the Wolds. Population is sparse and Howden, with its highly unusual church, is the only town of any size, though there is an easy cycle link to Goole, which adds extra accommodation options if you are looking to stay the night in the area. Village services become more frequent and wide-ranging as you reach such pretty settlements as Brantingham and Welton at the southern tip of the Yorkshire Wolds. Walkers' and cyclists' routes diverge for considerable distances, walkers more often following the River Ouse's banks. The going is flat, with wide vistas over the river and huge fields.

River Derwent at Barmby on the Marsh

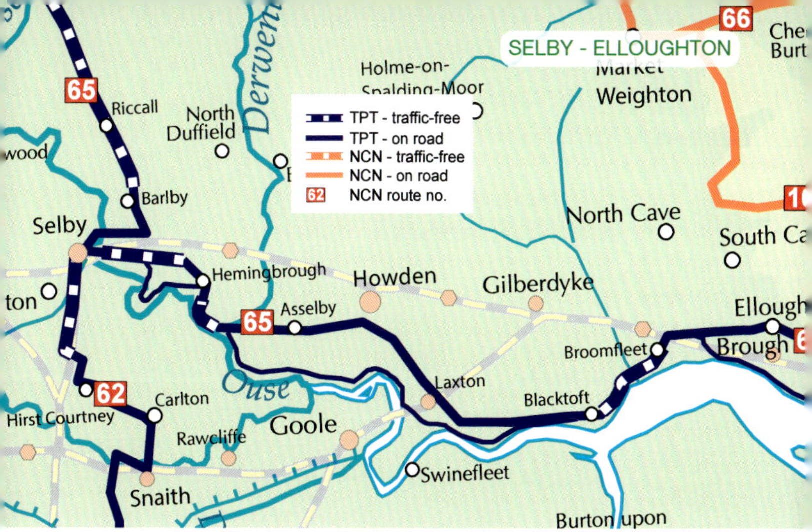

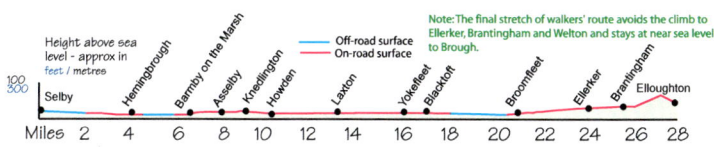

Cross the river Ouse and leave Selby

Howden Minster

Don't Miss

• **Howden Minster (Parish Church of St Peter & St Paul)** is not only one of East Yorkshire's finest churches but also one of its finest ruins.

It was built by the Prince Bishops of Durham in the middle ages to serve Howdenshire but suffered badly after the Reformation when the townspeople kept the nave as their parish church, leaving the east end to fall into ruin.

The 14th century ruined part backs onto the market square, indeed you can sit outside the Badger & Bear cafe and admire it.

The interior is also open to visitors and contains carvings by 'Mousey' Thompson of Kilburn and also some fine tombstone effegies.

Route Notes

1 Just over the swing bridge in Selby head R and follow the river Ouse on your right. The unsurfaced path becomes an excellent concrete track.

2 Walking route splits off R by Turnham Hall, along the top of the riverbank dyke. The riverbank dyke is easily followed all the way to Boothferry Bridge; it does continue on the dyke here though its course is a little less obvious as it passes houses.

3 In Hemingbrough exit the main street R onto Landing Lane. Pick up the singletrack bridleway beneath the river dyke at the end of it (joining the walking route).

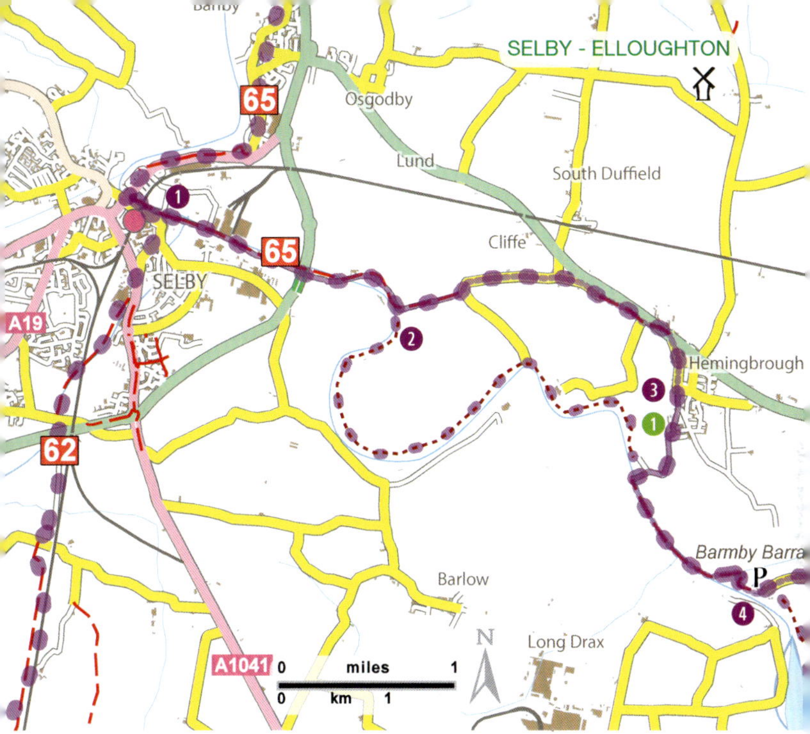

SELBY - ELLOUGHTON

4 Cross the mouth of the Derwent over the lock gates at this picturesque spot. The walking route again splits off to the R at Barmby Barrage car park, onto a grassy dyke-top path.

1 HEMINGBROUGH
Main street has a Londis minimart, Momma Brown's Artisan Bakery and a couple of pubs.

Leaving Hemingbrough

① Walking route passes under Boothferry Bridge then the huge and visually impressive M62 bridge.

★ *Howden*
See *Don't Miss* for Howden Minster. The Market Place is attractive and the Shire Hall here even has its own cinema.

① **WELLINGTON HOTEL**
31 Bridgegate, Howden DN14 7JG
01430 430258   oldmillbrewery.co.uk

② **PREMIER INN GOOLE**
Rawcliffe Road, Airmyn, Goole DN14 8JS
0333 003 1683   premierinn.com

③ **BRIARCROFT HOTEL**
Clifton Gardens, Goole DN14 6AR
01405 763024

④ **SALTMARSHE HALL (LUXURY)**
Saltmarshe DN14 7RX
01430 434920   saltmarshehall.com

① **KINGS HEAD PUB**, Barmby, does take away fish & chips.

② **BLACK SWAN**, Asselby

③ **HOWDEN** has many eating opportunities including the attractively located Badger & Bear cafe right by the minster ruins. Friday market at the Shire Hall.

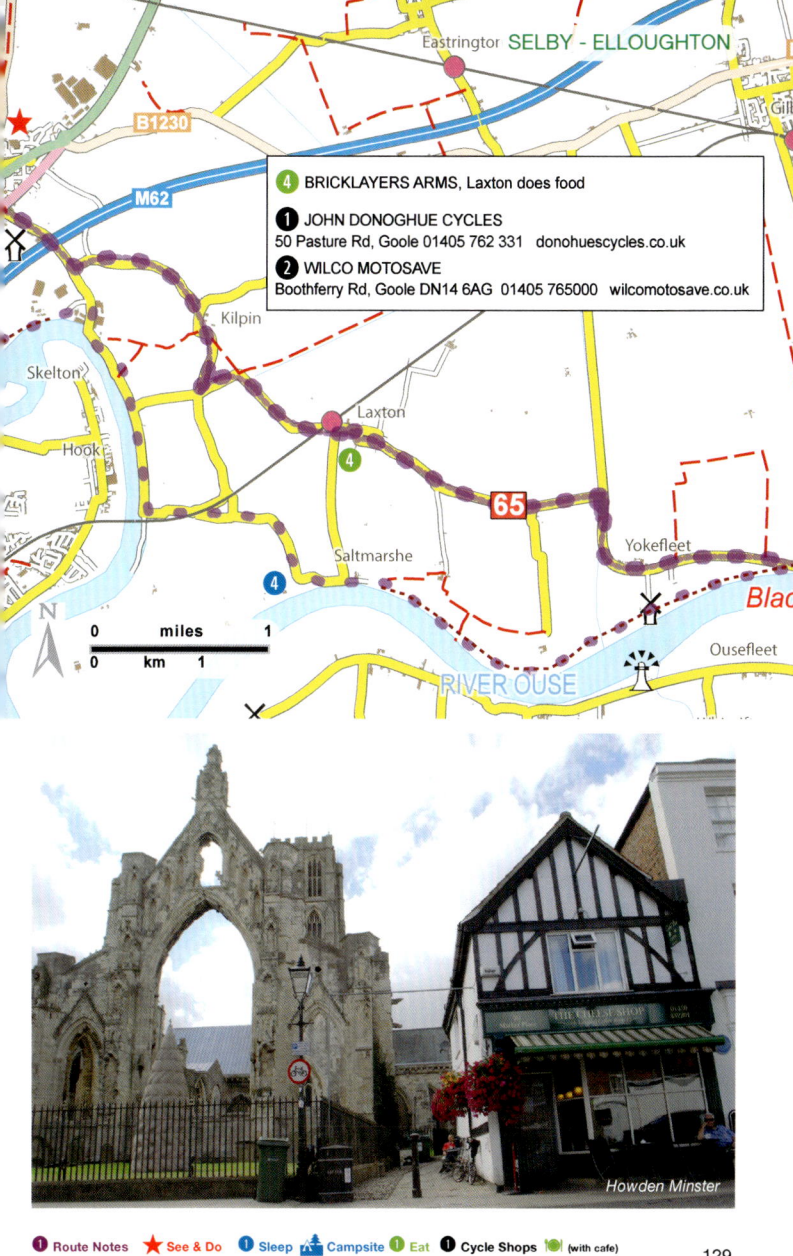

SELBY - ELLOUGHTON

4 BRICKLAYERS ARMS, Laxton does food

1 JOHN DONOGHUE CYCLES
50 Pasture Rd, Goole 01405 762 331   donohuecycles.co.uk

2 WILCO MOTOSAVE
Boothferry Rd, Goole DN14 6AG 01405 765000 wilcomotosave.co.uk

Howden Minster

① In Ellerker turn L after playground and L again. (Main route misses village centre which has a lovely big green ideal for picnics). From here the route through Brantingham to Elloughton is straightforward.

⭐ *Wolds Villages*

Though this lovely little collection of wolds villages is light on services (with the exception of Elloughton), they are attractive places to meander through.

Ellerker is a lovely village centred around one of the biggest village greens you will see anywhere, backed by some grand houses and bordered by a tiny clear brook. Brantingham is perhaps quaintest of all, with its brick terraces decorated with wooden porches. The village pond is backed by estate land. The elaborate war memorial was built from parts of the old Victorian Town Hall in Hull.

⭐ *Blacktoft Jetty*

Important for ships travelling up the Ouse to Goole; it's a handy laying up point to wait at until the tide has risen enough for them to go on. Ships from all countries dock here, especially from the Baltic area.

① CAVE CASTLE HOTEL
Church Hill South Cave HU15 2EU
01420 422245   cavecastlehotel.com

② TRAVELODGE HULL SOUTH CAVE
A63 Eastbound, Beacon Services,
South Cave HU15 1SA
08719 846147   travelodge.co.uk

🛖 TRINITY CAMPING SITE
The Old Vicarage, Blacktoft DN14 7YW
01430 441751   campingandcaravanningclub.co.uk

SELBY - ELLOUGHTON

1 BLACKTOFT Old School Hall with tea making facilities and second hand books.

? WESTEND CAFE 30 West End, South Cave

2 BLACK HORSE RESTAURANT at Ellerker. Evening menu & Sunday lunch.

3 TRITON INN, Brantingham open for lunch and dinner.

4 ELLOUGHTON has bar meals at the Half Moon and Julies cafe and a local shop.

5 BROUGH has plenty of eating opportunities, including cafes and pubs.

TPT GUIDE

Elloughton & Brough - Hornsea

Route Info

26 miles / 42 km
Off - road - 15 miles / 24 km
Height Ascended 105m / 345ft
Above figures are for shortest route option only

Both walking and cycling routes pass under the truly spectacular Humber Bridge. Past the bridge the walking route maintains its course along the Humber, whilst the cycling route branches off through Hessle and onto Hull centre. Through the grand old port of Hull you head on to the quiet and easy Hornsea Rail Trail, whose unsealed, earth surface is largely access barrier free and leads through agricultural countryside to the resort of Hornsea, with its traditional seaside food and entertainments. Accommodation planning may be different for walkers, cyclists and horse riders, as the various user route options are separated by up to 2 miles in some places.

Shark sculpture at Hull's The Deep

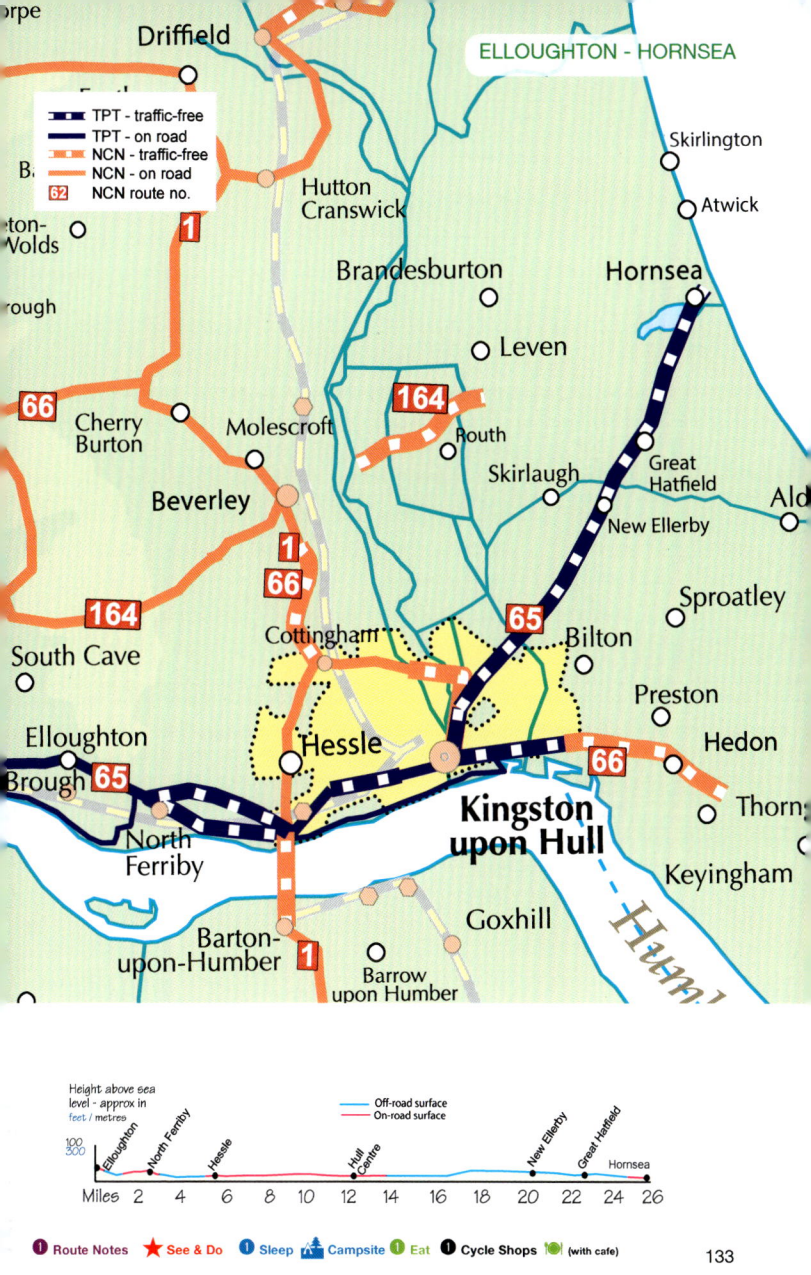

TPT GUIDE

Cycle or walk over the magnificent Humber Bridge

Don't Miss

• Follow NCN 1 signs onto the cycle path across the **Humber Bridge** for a unique bird's eye view of the estuary and to get a true appreciation of one of the world's longest single span suspension bridges at over 2000m.

• **Hull's Deep** is hugely popular and opened as the world's only submarium (you can walk under the huge main tank). It houses a unique blend of interactives and stunning aquaria. Home to thousands of fish and many sharks, rays and penguins. Great views of the Humber estuary from the restaurant.

ELLOUGHTON - HORNSEA

- **Hull's Victoria Square and Museums** Queen Victoria Square acts as a focal point for the meeting of old and new in Hull. Surrounding the square are the a fine collection of civic attractions.
The Martime Museum here is undergoing a thorough restoration with the aim of bringing much of it back into the condition it was when it opened in 1871. Spring 2025 should see visitors able to explore Hull's history of whaling in Greenland and its fishing industry amongst much else. The Ferens Art Gallery is one of the finest regional art galleries and includes European Old Masters from the sixteenth century onwards and twentieth-century British art.
City Hall hosts all manner of live perfromances and ceremonies and the main hall has a floor, balcony and gallery with total capacity for 1,200 people seated,

TPT GUIDE

- **Hull's Old Town, Fruit Market and Marina** are conveniently linked by Princes Dock Street and the wonderful Murdoch Connection foot and cycle bridge (named after a pioneering local female GP). The Fruit Market tells you the area's history but the recent focus has been post industrial rejuvenation with bars and cafes springing up alongside fine old pubs such the Minerva which borders the Marnia and the huge Humber Estuary. The Old Town is packed with wonderful old buildings with highlights being Hepworth's Arcade, Hull Minster and the Museums Quarter (Wilberforce, Transport and East Riding museums plus the huge trawling vessel the Arctic Corsair).

ELLOUGHTON - HORNSEA

- **Burton Constable Hall** is a grand Elizabethan House with over 200 acres of Capability Brown parkland. Beautiful collections in the house and the chance for refreshment at the Stable tearooms. The Cabinet of Curiosities is a room containing all manner of things (even in 1769 William Constable still believed that it was possible to cross breed rabbits and chickens, as is revealed in his correspondence here...)

- **Hornsea Mere & Wassand Hall** The mere is a lovely walking spot and also the largest freshwater lake in Yorkshire. Offers boating and a cafe too. Wassand Hall is open on selected days and tea in the walled garden is a highlight.

- Journey's End at **Hornsea Seafront** means the chance to pose in front of the iconic sculpture there, known as the Seamark (like the one at Southport), and then to meander along the front with its seaside cheer and cafes.

1. FERRIBY'S COFFEE HOUSE
27 Low Street, North Ferriby

2. THE COUNTRY PARK INN
Cliff Road, Hessle

3. HESSLE
Lots of choice including the attractive Marquis of Granby pub.

1 In Elloughton centre go L at crossroads by church then L up Dale Rd, crossing over the A63, bend R then turn R onto High Rd and climb to a viewpoint over the Humber.

2 Following TPT signs at Welton bypasses the pretty village to your R, which is worth a look.

3 Turn R down Lowfield La and L alongside main road. Cross main road on ramped bridge and carry on alongside A63 on path. Under tunnel and L.

4 Roadside option to Hessle Pass Duke of Cumberland pub and straight on at junction. Follow cycle paths around road junctions to turn R down Ferriby Rd. Turn R into Humber Bridge Country Park and follow signs on demarcated lanes past car park. Follow signs onto woodland path, exiting onto narrow Cliff Top Lane (cycle foreshore option joins here).

5 Foreshore to Hessle Pass Duke of Cumberland pub and R at junction onto Church Road. This leads through pretty North Ferriby to wonderful section alongside the Humber.

6 Walking Route Option At Hessle foreshore the walking route splits off R, down Jeans Walk, using the Wolds Way. It is virtually unsigned for much of its length, though self-evident, largely following the northern shore of the massive Humber estuary. The most spectacular section heads over the roofs of the depots at the Port of Hull and across the massive lock gates at the entrance to Albert Dock.

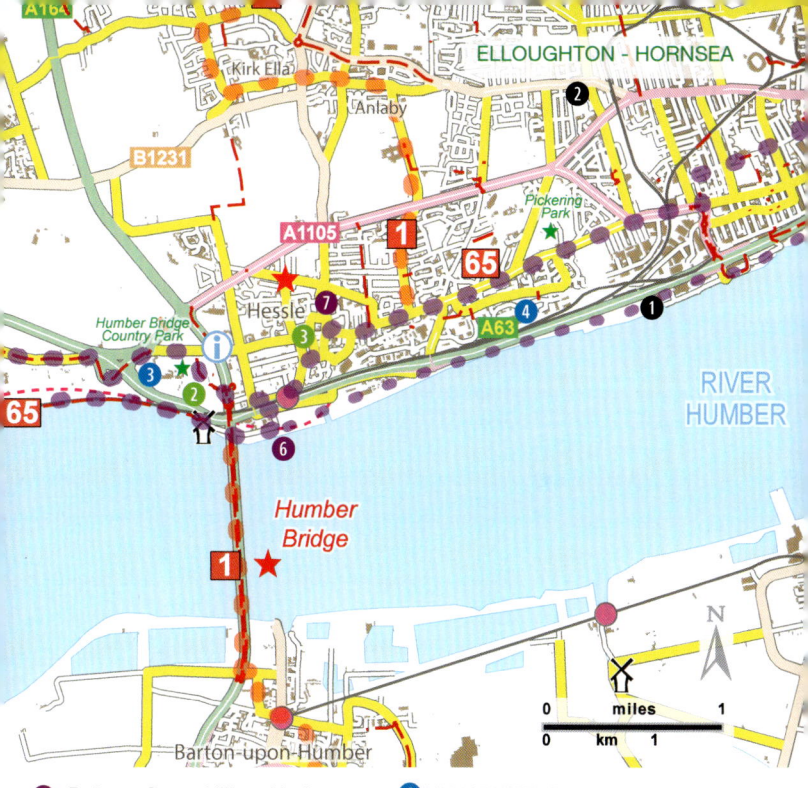

7 R down Grove Hill and L down Southgate then R at major junction onto Hessle Road. Out of Hessle you are following the main Hessle to Hull road. The roadside cycle lanes can be tricky to understand, but essetially you follow this main road.

1 GREEN DRAGON 🍴
Cowgate, Welton HU15 1NB
01482 666700 greendragonpubwelton.co.uk

2 EASTDALE B&B
3 Melton Bottom, Melton HU14 3HU
01482 632870 eastdale-bed-and-breakfast.co.uk

3 PREMIER INN HULL WEST
Ferriby Road, Hessle HU13 0JA
0333 003 1733 premierinn.com

4 VILLAGE HOTEL CLUB HULL
Henry Boot Way, HU4 7DY
01482 427110 village-hotels.co.uk

1 HALFORDS
Unit 2 St Andrew's Quay
Hull HU3 4SA

2 JOBES CYCLES
749-753 Anlaby Road, Hull HU4 6DJ
01482 568398

● Route Notes ★ See & Do ● Sleep ▲ Campsite ● Eat ● Cycle Shops 🍴 (with cafe)

① Cycling Route Option
The route into Hull weaves its way along numerous back streets after leaving the main Hessle Hull Road. Note the ornate fountain at junction of Gordon Street and The Boulevard.

② Cross Mount Pleasant and follow NCN 65 & 66 signed Bransholme, Sutton & Hornsea.

③ 2km (1.3 miles) out of Hull split right onto NCN 65 as NCN66 carries on. Easy to miss.

★ The Deep
See Don't Miss pg134.

★ The Humber Estuary & the Port of Hull
The Humber Estuary holds lots of wildlife and you get great views of it around the Hessle foreshore at the Humber Bridge. It is home to ancient sea lamphreys, a strange looking fish some 200 million years older than the dinosaurs. There are also large populations of grey seals and migrating birds.

★ Victoria Dock Heritage Trail
The walking route to ferry uses part of this. Heritage signs detail the interesting remainders of the huge docks here that once saw such spectacles as live cattle imports.

ELLOUGHTON - HORNSEA

① EARLSMERE HOTEL
76 – 78 Sunny Bank HU3 1LQ
01482 341977   earlsmerehotel.co.uk

See overleaf for following on map

② ROYAL HOTEL HULL
170 Ferensway HU1 3UF
0871 222 1094   britanniahotels.com

③ TRAVELODGE HULL CENTRAL
Pryme Street HU2 8HR
08719 846473   travelodge.co.uk

④ HOTEL IBIS HULL CENTRE
Osbourne Street HU1 2NL
01482 947950   all.accor.com

⑤ HOLIDAY INN HULL MARINA
Castle Street HU1 2BX
01482 692600   ihg.com

⑥ PREMIER INN HULL CITY CENTRE
Tower Street HU9 1TQ
0333 003 1731   premierinn.com

❶ CLIFF PRATT LTD
61 Spring Bank, Hull HU3 1AG
01482 228293   cpcycles.com

❷ R-EVOLUTION
Market Place, Hull HU1 1RH
07869 680943   r-evolution.org.uk
Secure parking and e-bike hire

❸ HALFORDS
4B Clough Road Retail Park, Hull HU6 7PT

❹ EVANS CYCLES
Craven Street North, Mount Pleasant HU9 2AP
0343 9092900   evanscycles.com

Ⓜ REPAIR2RIDE
Mobike service covering Hull and much of East Yorkshire
07957 026 262   repair2ride.co.uk

Paragon Interchange also provides 160 spaces for cycles in a two-tier rack, 6 of which allow those with E-bikes to charge up their bicycles in the safety of the cycle hub. It is located in the main train station.

The walking route near The Deep gives magnificent views back up the Humber

● Route Notes   ★ See & Do   ● Sleep   ▲ Campsite   ● Eat   ● Cycle Shops   ◉ (with cafe)

① **Walking Route Options** At Hull Marina R past Minerva pub takes you along the front to cross the River Hull and end up at The Deep, whilst L heads up the east side of the marina, across Murdoch's Connection bridge, Castle St and onto Princes Dock St. to take you to the centre.

★ *The Deep* See Don't Miss page 134)

★ *Ye OldeBlack Boye pub* (former pipeshop / brothel!)
★ *Ferens Art Gallery*
From old masters to contemporary paintings
★ *Streetlife Museum of Transport*
★ *Arctic Corsair*
Britain's last sidewinder trawler
★ *Lightship*
Once a navigation aid on the Humber Estuary
★ *Murdoch's Connection* Spectacular cycle bridge

★ **Wilberforce House**
Birthplace of the famous anti-slave trade campaigner, now a museum to his memory and has relics of the cruel business he helped ban, such as leg-irons, whips and chains His statue stands overlooking Queens Gardens

★ *Maritime Museum (reopening 2025)*
Covers centuries of maritime history, including whaling voyages to Spitsbergen and the art scrimshaw (sailors' delicate whalebone carvings)

1 HULL
A huge choice of eateries with pleasant sit out cafes by the Marina.

❶ Route Notes ★ See & Do ❶ Sleep ⛺ Campsite ❶ Eat ❶ Cycle Shops (with cafe)

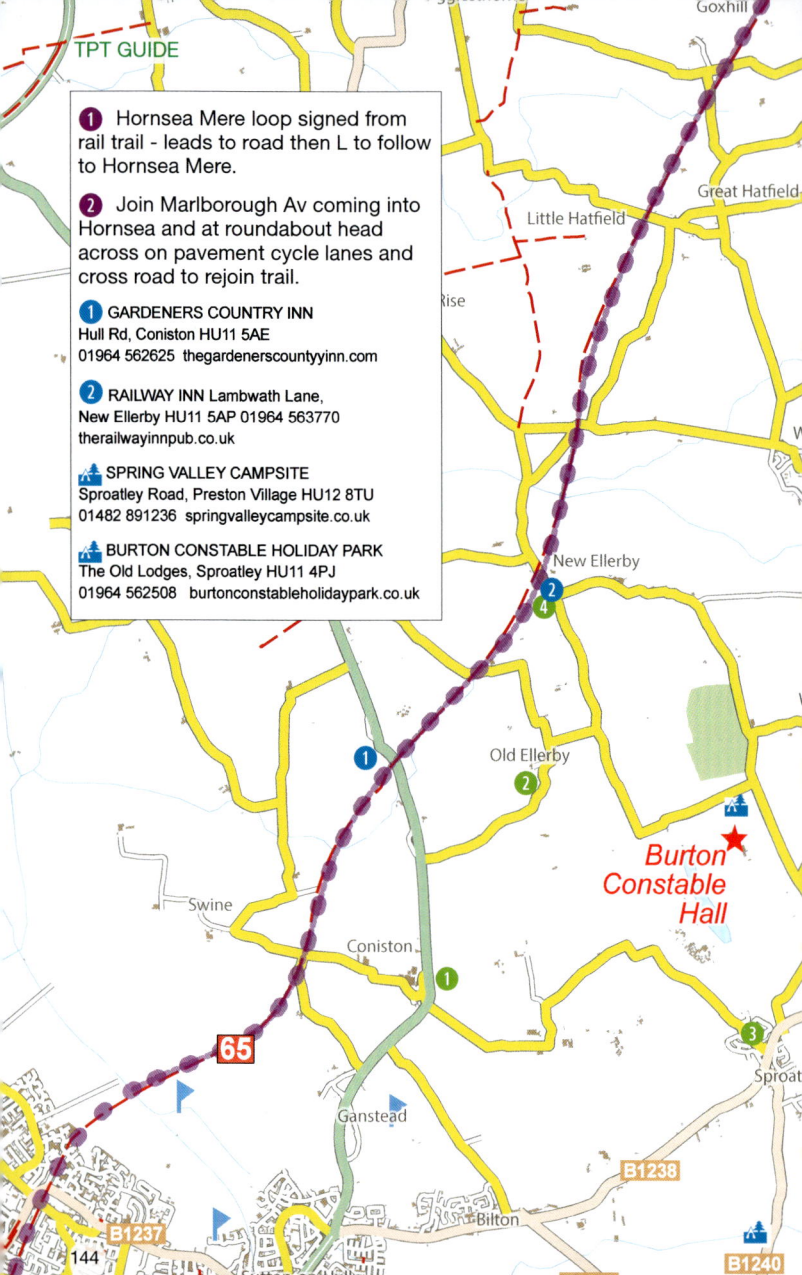

ELLOUGHTON – HORNSEA

1 SHARK EBIKES
Unit 8, Southgate Court
Old Bridge Rd HU18 1RP
0560 364 3858
sharkebikes.com

★ *Burton Constable Hall*
See Don't Miss pg 135

1 CONISTON Farm shop has coffee machine and the Blacksmiths Arms pub here does food

2 BLUEBELL INN Old Ellerby

3 SPROATLEY Pub meals At Constable Arms and Blue Bell.

4 RAILWAY INN New Ellerby

5 FALCON Withernwick Pub meals

3 NORTHORPE CAMPSITE / B&B
Atwick Road, Hornsea HU18 1EJ
01964 534063   northorpehornsea.co.uk

GOXHILL MEADOWS GLAMPING
Glebe Farm House, Goxhill Lane
Goxhill, HU11 5RW   0747 012 5121
goxhillmeadows.co.uk

WOOD LAKE CAMPSITE
Mappleton Road, Great Hatfield HU11 4UP
01964 536869
woodlakecampsite.co.uk

WHITE COTTAGE HOLIDAY PARK
Hull Road, Seaton HU11 5RN
07740 918499
whitecottageholidaypark.co.uk

CHURCH VIEW CAMPSITE
Norton, Church Lane, Atwick YO25 8DH
07804 851666
campingandcaravanningclub.co.uk

1 Route Notes   ★ See & Do   Sleep   Campsite   **1** Eat   **1** Cycle Shops   (with cafe)

TPT GUIDE

Hornsea

Sandy beach fronts promenade with traditional seaside attractions. Town centre has attractive buildings.

★ *Wassand Hall* 🍽

Opens for selected days throughout the year. Lovely Regency style house and also drinks and wonderful cakes in the beautiful walled gardens. Wassand Estate owns much of the land to the south of Hornsea Mere and runs it as conservation land, with breeding marsh harriers visible and also fine walks with views over the mere.

★ *Hornsea Mere* 🍽

Yorkshire's largest freshwater lake. Bird reserve plus boating and fishing.

★ *Hornsea Museum*

Museum of local life.

★ *Hornsea Freeport*

Shopping outlet and Bugtopia Hornsea Zoo

★ *Potter About Hornsea*

Public art trail depicting Hornsea Pottery's iconic designs through a series of artworks

★ *Bettisons Folly*

Built so that the servant of 19th century Hull brewer, William Bettison, could see his master return from work and prepare his dinner in time!

❶ THE VICTORIA
39 Market Place HU18 1AN
01964 211122

❷ ADMIRALTY GUEST HOUSE
7 Marine Drive HU18 1NJ
01964 536414   admiraltyguesthouse.co.uk

❸ ASHBURNAM
1 Victoria Avenue HU18 1NH
01964 535118
ashburnamguesthouse.co.uk

❹ MERLSTEAD HOUSE
59 Eastgate HU18 1NB
07868 746832
merlstead-house.yorkshire-hotel.com

❶ HORNSEA

Lots of options along Newbegin from traditional cafes to Asian restaurants. In the town and along the front there are the traditional fish & chip and other seaside eateries and at the far northern end the traditional and very pleasant Floral Hall Cafe. King of the fish & chips has to be Sullivans.

Hornsea's attractive main street, Newbegin

Equestrian Information

Horse Stabling

Godley Stud Riding School
Green Lane
Gee Cross
Hyde
SK14 3BD
0161 366 9103
www.godleystudridingschool.com

Hargate Hill Equestrian Centre
Hargate Hill
Glossop
SK13 6JL
01457 865518
www.hargatehill.com

Pikenaze Farm
Woodhead
Glossop
SK13 1JD
01457 861577

Mallard House Riding Centre
Finkle Street
Wortley
S35 7DH
0114 288 7743

Rockley Equestrian Centre
Rockley Lane
Worsbrough, Barnsley
S75 3DS
01709 887766
rockleyequestrian.co.uk

Bradwell Equestrian
Folly Farm
Thurlstone
S36 7QF
07701 046700

Whincover Farm Livery Stables
Golden Smithies Lane
Wath-upon-Dearne
S63 7ES
07788 103409
www.whincoverfarm-liverystables.co.uk

Mill Lane Stables
Mill Lane
Brayton
Selby
YO8 9LB
01757 702940
www.mill-lane-stables.co.uk

Naburn Grange Riding Centre
Naburn
York
YO19 4RU
01904 728283
www.adveb.co.uk/naburn/

Oxmardyke Equestrian Centre
Tongue Lane
Gilberdyke
HU15 2UY
07961 104690
www.oxmardyke-equestrian-centre.co.uk

Vets

Churchfields Vets
Heeley Inn Farm,
Barnsley Road
Hoylandswaine
S36 8AA
01226 733333
01226 763542 (equine unit)
www.churchfieldvets.co.uk

Keep up to date with the TPT at

www.transpenninetrail.org.uk

- Trail news
- Become a TPT friend or ranger
- Family info
- Buy the official printed maps
- Get in touch
- Detailed maps of access controls
- Horseriders guides
- Souvenirs & posters

And much more!

Map 1 Irish Sea - Yorkshire
Map 2 Derbyshire & Yorkshire
Map 3 Yorkshire - North Sea

Introducing the new Eos tandem by Circe Cycles
......stylish, versatile and made for adventure

Fully belt drive compatible

•

Low step through frame design

•

Specially designed carbon tandem fork with thru axle

•

24" and 26" wheel size options for tyre widths 25 to 50mm

•

Compatible with Circe's Separable System and Traveller flight case

circecycles.com | +44 (0)1954 782020

Airnimal **JOEY**

WITH YOU FOR THE JOURNEY

Now compatible with 24" and 26" wheel sizes

www.airnimal.co
+44 (0)1954 782020

Airnimal
High performance folding bikes

TRANS PENNINE TRAIL IN PHOTOS

Barnsley Canal near Royston (below) & Upper Don Trail near Penistone (above)